Ralph Lauren The man, the vision, the style

Ralph Lauren The man, the vision, the style

Colin McDowell

contents

introduction

When, in July 1998, Smithsonian's National Museum of American History decided to preserve the original Star-Spangled Banner—for almost two centuries the symbol of a nation's pride, sewn in the eighteenth century by Mary Pickersgrill—it seemed entirely appropriate that the honor of donating $13 million should fall to Ralph Lauren. The flag was the inspiration for the national anthem of Francis Scott Key, and it is the quintessential symbol of America and what being American means to its many citizens. Generations have proudly stood tall before it, reaffirming their belief in what it stands for.

It was appropriate because Ralph Lauren has also come to stand for much of what Americans and the rest of the world consider important aspects of his country's culture and life. He has done so by largely ignoring the vagaries of fashion change. Refreshingly, he has separated dress from the tyranny of fashion dictatorship. He has looked specifically at what makes American fashion not only different but unique: sportswear, casual elegance, the luxury of simplicity married to the highest level of workmanship and the very best of fabrics and materials—and he has emphasized the timelessness inherent in it. The man who says of fashion that he has no time at all 'for the that baloney' is clearly a man who has roots deeper than those normally found in fashion's shallow soil. Ralph Lauren's clothes exemplify the greatest confidence of all—the confidence to simplify, leave unadorned and allow to speak clearly, directly and honestly as all good design in whatever field must.

In a period when fashion is frequently ageist, Ralph Lauren's clothes find an answering cord in the hearts of minds of people all over the world—

because of their universality. Wearing them, the sixty-year-old mother can stand proud next to her thirty-five-year-old daughter and neither will feel embarrassed. A father and his college-kid son can go off fishing in almost identical clothes and each will be dressed appropriately for his age. That is the power and achievement of Ralph Lauren. He is the man who first gave international cachet to the weft and warp of American life; its history, geography and culture; and he has done so in the most direct and effective of ways—through people's appearance and, through that, their self-esteem.

But the skills of Ralph Lauren are not confined to clothes alone. He has taught us how to create our surroundings, he has educated our taste and he has revolutionized the way we shop. When preparing this book I was given unprecedented co-operation by Ralph: extensive interviews with him, his staff and his family were augmented by unrestricted access to his archives and, greatest privilege of all, visits to all his houses. I am very grateful for the trust placed in me by Ralph and those close to him during this project, especially as his generosity came with no 'strings'. Neither he nor anyone involved with him has asked me to alter or modify anything I've written. As he frequently told me, 'this is your book, not mine'. I hope that what follows makes all those who have been so generous with their time feel that I have captured some at least of the illusive and multi-faceted talents know as Ralph Lauren because in one important point Ralph is wrong: this is his book, not only because it is about him but also because his protean genius created everything of which I write.

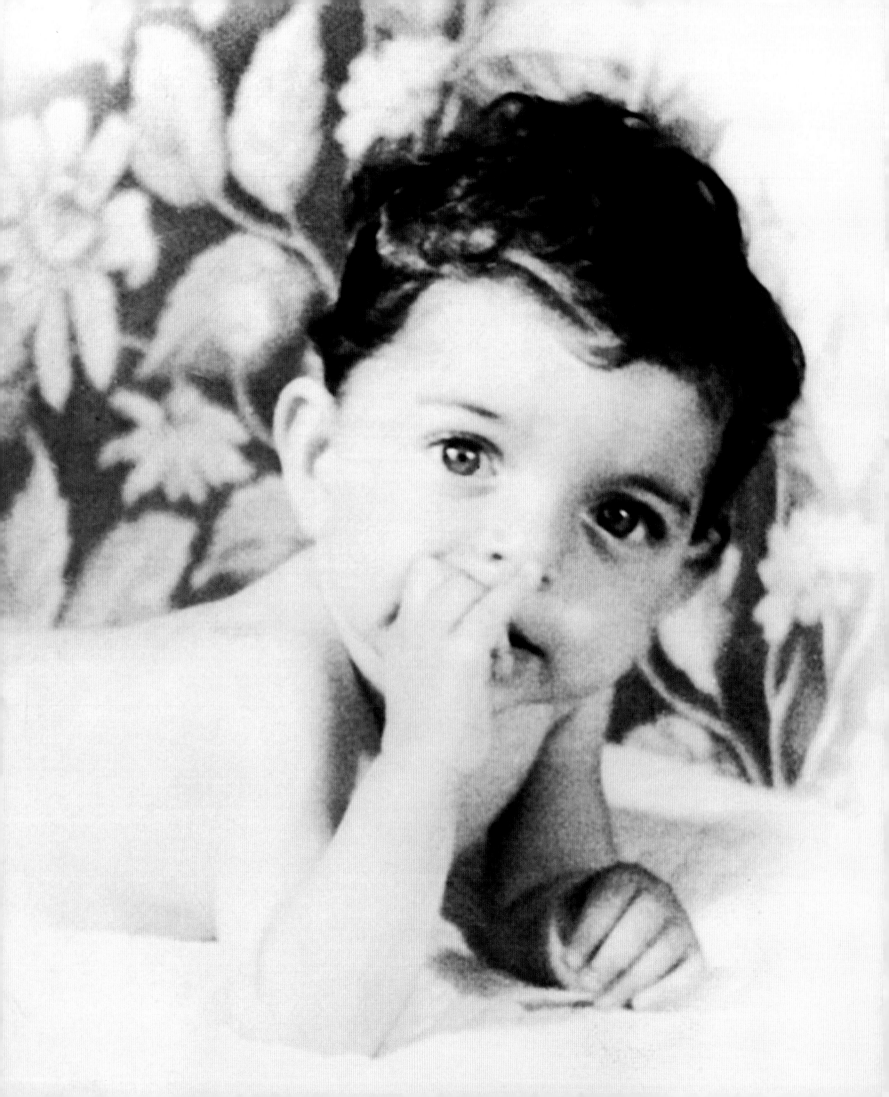

beginnings

In global terms October 14, 1939, was not the most auspicious date to be born. The conflict that would soon escalate into World War II had already begun in Europe. Although it would be two years before the United States was drawn totally into the conflict as a result of the attack on Pearl Harbor in December 1941, the whole country was aware that what was happening across the Atlantic—and especially in Poland—could not be dismissed as some little local difficulty.

And yet at Ralph Lauren's birth, his parents had every reason for hope. Russian Jews, they had, like thousands of other immigrants to the United States, managed to survive the bad years of the thirties and could feel secure that they were bringing up their family in the safest place in the world—a country largely at peace with itself, ready to take advantage of the new prosperity that was clearly on its way and as yet unaware of the social and ethnic problems that would hit it in the following 25 years. Further, they were living not only in the land of opportunity but in New York, the city of opportunity. It had proved a good place for Frank and Frieda Lifshitz, a place that had given them stability and enabled them to raise a family to which Ralph was the latest—and, indeed, the last—addition. His sister Thelma had been born in 1930, his brothers Leonard and Jerome in 1932 and 1934 respectively.

Ralph Lauren admits that his background was totally normal, even ordinary. In contrast to the clichéd image of a young designer who as a child pored over mommy's copies of *Vogue,* when he was a boy he was playing stickball with the rest of the guys.

"For Ralph, even at a young age it was the image that mattered … he would put powder in his hair to make himself look like some movie star …"

No more interested in fashion than any of his family, he was just a regular, everyday, straight-up-and-down New York kid, a product of the Bronx, living within a secure family environment poised at the middle point of the artisanal curve. His father made his living as a house painter. Remembered by his son as a man of considerable artistic talent, he was a craftsman-painter, called in to add finesse to public buildings by creating special surface treatments such as wood-grain or faux-marble effects. He also painted murals, and several New York buildings from the thirties and forties once boasted his work in their lobbies. "My father was an artist," Ralph says, "but he had a family to feed. He had to take the work that situations offered him." The Laurens lived in the Mosholu Parkway section of the Bronx where trees grew in the streets and the Botanical Garden was only a short walk away. Ralph's childhood companion and lifelong friend Steve Bell remembers their apartment in a walk-up where, as visitors came near the door, they could always smell cooking. "It made it such a warm, nice place to be," he says. "Frieda was a very good cook. Very Jewish traditional. I used to go up and get Ralph ready to go to school, because he lived right next door to the schoolyard. He was never ready. He couldn't find his socks or he had to sit and have his breakfast. I can see Frieda now—she was a very pretty woman incidentally, small and round—she used to make breakfast for us. She would apologize because they got kosher milk delivered with the cream on the top and she would say, 'Stevie, I'm sorry. I have to give Ralph the cream. He was so skinny—a real skinny little kid.'"

"Ralph loved his parents. He was incredibly proud of his father. He would say, 'I wanna show you what my father did' and we'd go into these lobbies of office blocks and see the textured walls Frank had done. Even then, Jerry was Ralph's best friend. He was our idol. He was just old enough for us not to be competitive with him. We looked up to him, because he always went out with these great-looking girls. All us guys were ball players. We just played ball all the time. Ralph and I weren't just rivals. We were world-class rivals. He had no interest in school work. We used to have a geometry class together in high school. It was comical. He used to sit next to me. In fact, he was virtually in the same chair. When Miss Lowey used to call on him he would say 'Steve, help me!' I couldn't help him. I was just as bad. No, school just wasn't his focus."

Steve Bell remembers the Lifshitz home on Stueben Avenue as being typical of most in the neighborhood: "We lived right next to each other. His parents were terrific. Although my family were Italian, not Jewish, I was always made to feel at home. The apartment was small. Maybe the entire space was around a thousand square feet. But it was always very comfortable, even though it was crowded. It had a warm atmosphere. Thelma used to have to sleep on a pull-out. Of course, she and Lenny were so much older; by the time Ralph was a teenager they were gone. Then Ralph shared the bedroom with Jerry—just as I did with my brother."

The forties were a golden time in the US, especially for those like the Lifshitzes lucky enough to live in a close-knit community within an exciting city which offered daily challenges and rewards. Of course, such a city can be daunting and it is true that Ralph Lauren's parents were both more inclined to look inward than outward, to cling to the family as the true core unit of existence, to put hearth and home at the center of life. Very much conscious of their own culture and the importance of maintaining it as the strongest thing they could pass on to their children, they had met in their late teens at a social club expressly set up to maintain Russian culture. They spoke

Above left: Ralph, contemplating a
future life in the sun?
Above right: Ralph at one of his favorite
childhood places—the baseball field.

Yiddish together—with, Jerry Lauren recalls, "a few Russian phrases thrown in"—and were both Orthodox, being regular attendees at synagogue. As is often the case with such families, it was Frieda, the earth-mother figure, who mainly made it her business to keep alive the Jewish culture and religion that meant so much to her. A strong woman, she protected the Lifshitz family life, building and nurturing it as if the outside world barely existed. Her home was her world, her family the only thing that mattered to her, apart from her religion.

World War II united the US like nothing else in the twentieth century. As men began to be drafted overseas, family values became paramount. Wartime hits—"I'll Get By," "Ma, I Miss Your Apple Pie," even "White Christmas,"—were threnodies for a world of lost innocence and security. Men in dugouts in far lands longed for the security and warmth of their girl, their home, mom, pop, and the kids. Those waiting at home took refuge in escapist movies like *Woman of the Year*, starring Katharine Hepburn and Spencer Tracy together for the first time, and *Mrs. Miniver*, with Greer Garson. It was only after the war that its human cost was questioned.

Life continued to be good in material terms. The average family income in New York City in 1938 was in the region of $2,760 a year. By 1942 it was over $4,000. No wonder that, in their modest way, Frank and Frieda Lifshitz felt increasingly at home as they joined with the whole neighborhood in the war effort. Belief in family, trust in religion, putting the needs of the US first: these were the bedrock values of how they planned to bring up their children.

Ralph Lauren was just coming up to six years old when the atom bomb dropped on Hiroshima, thereby putting an abrupt end to the hostilities with Japan that had continued after the defeat of Hitler in Europe. He was about old enough to take advantage of what the world's most advanced consumer society could offer for entertainment. The copywriter of a toothpaste ad of the time might have had the young Ralph in mind when he wrote "This is an American child. This is an American home. Lucky young American. No child in the world has so bright a future."

Ralph was not thinking too far ahead though. There was quite enough of the here and now to engage him. The New York Yankees, for example, or hanging out with his friends. One of the best things that happened to Ralph as a boy was sharing a bedroom with his brothers Jerry and Lenny. Five-and-a-half and seven years older than him respectively, they were, by the standards of the guys in his gang, the last word in sophistication. Because of their relative ages it was with Jerry that Ralph became really close, so much so that, as Jerry explains, "The five years' difference never meant anything to either of us when we were kids. We played together, we imagined together, we created together, and we shared common interests. I did feel like the older brother as we grew older. I felt like he had to be protected. But we were really good friends. There was never any conflict, except the sort of family quarrels all boys enjoy."

Most quarrels concerned sport, Ralph's prime interest as a child and one that has barely diminished throughout his life. He loved the boastful banter he had with his brothers about the top players—and he loved even more being able to repeat their comments to his friends, with all the confidence of superior knowledge. As Jerry says, "He watched me and Lenny as we grew up but it was me he watched most closely because of our ages. I guess I must have been a role model for Ralph but he realized things pretty fast. Always at home he was very quiet. Quietly observing. We were all artistic. Always sketching. Thelma was very good. I wasn't bad. My mother would pay me ten dollars to do a sketch of somebody in the family. Ralph didn't sketch so much but he took it all in."

Above left: Ralph, after he left the army.
Above right: Ralph, stylish at a young
age and looking to the future.

One of the good things about being the last-born is that it can bring out a determination not to be cowed by older members of the family, the desire to shine and hold your own, the need to develop the character to know when to fight and when to yield in family rivalries. Ralph learned soon enough and, taking his knowledge out of the house and into the playground, he used it in such a way that he soon became a sort of leader in his group of boys, even though they were so tightly welded as to need no real leader. A more accurate description might be that Ralph was a leading light in a gang of boys whose subsequent careers and even pre-eminence in their fields suggests that they were perhaps exceptional in their spirit, their drive, and their determination to make something of themselves.

The young Ralph Lauren gave his heart and soul to baseball, hero-worshiping the New York Yankees and longing more than anything in the world to grow up good enough to make the major leagues, a dream with which millions of men who cast their minds back will identify and understand. This was not to be. Ultimately Ralph was not tall enough to be a professional ball player but that did not weaken his passionate involvement with the game. Sport and the hero-worship of its great exponents are a natural rite of passage for boys the world over and Ralph Lauren was no exception. He and his friends had their special spot where they "chewed the fat," made outrageous claims for their heroes, denigrated the heroes of others, struggled, bantered and "horsed around" in a spirit of masculine camaraderie. The place was an iron fence, known as "the rail," and it was where the boys would talk about sports and, as they grew older, boast about usually non-existent sexual conquests. Each of the many neighborhood gangs had its own place on the rail, sanctioned by tradition and strenuously defended. As the evening's last insult hung in the air and they peeled off to their individual homes, or back to Ralph's, they had bonded as thoroughly as young puppies or cubs who hunt in a pack, think as a group, yet keep their individuality and need for dominance within the tight-knit social entity they make up.

Who were the heroes who made them care so desperately that for that brief period between boyhood and adolescence they seemed almost to live surrogate lives? In Ralph's case, it was pre-eminently Mickey Mantle, whose greatest season was 1956, when the teenage Ralph was probably at his most impressionable. As he says, "When I played baseball, I was Mickey. I played the game as he played the game and I thought the thoughts he would be thinking." Such total immersion in a character or a situation developed very easily in Ralph. Jerry recalls how, when he and Ralph were really young and had sword fights, they were never just children playing at having a sword fight. "He was, say, the Duke of York and I was some other duke. We were real people. And then, when we got boxing gloves and we used to have fights, I'd be Joe Louis and he would be Sugar Ray Robinson."

The place of Mickey Mantle in this surrogate role play is significant. Handsome and strong-jawed, he was exactly the sort of hero with whom the young Ralph Lauren would be expected to identify. As Jerry said, "For Ralph, even at a young age it was the image that mattered. When we used to play he would put powder in his hair to make himself look like some movie star—maybe Cary Grant. Then as we got older, Frank Sinatra came into our lives and he was the greatest influence. We copied everything we could about him. He really was Ralph's hero." Increasingly, clothes became important to both brothers, not because they were interested in fashion but

because they were interested in themselves. Ralph started feeling around for an image for himself based on what he saw as the great success of his older brother. Clothes were for making a guy look cool so that he could attract the girls. They were chosen to instill confidence—with the Lauren brothers just as with millions of adolescent boys across the globe. Ralph's interest was in how he personally should wear clothes to achieve the social status which, like most young men, he believed was linked to his appearance. In an often-quoted remark, he points out that as "the baby brother" many items of clothing came to him down the line from Lenny via Jerry and, for him, that gave them a credibility and talismanic quality that brand-new clothes did not have. Many were a special experience, like wearing a piece of family history. You don't need a crystal ball to see this as the beginning of the cultural approach that was to be the basis of the Polo Ralph Lauren empire, predicated as it is on the assumption that, while fashion is fickle, "real" clothes are better because they exemplify continuity. How many times has Ralph Lauren said that he responds to old, well-worn clothes and dislikes the concept of fashion because it presupposes newness? That is why, even though he found school irksome, he noticed and appreciated the slightly shabby jackets with leather patches on the sleeves worn by many of his teachers—a look he still frequently emulates by wearing vintage pieces.

Ralph would go with Jerry to places like Alexander's Discount Store or Discount of the Day and go through the racks of clothes trying to find something he could afford and that would make him look "dynamite." Jerry remembers, "Even if it was just some funny old leisure jacket, he always seemed to know what he wanted to do, how to wear it. He had a sense about himself." It was vanity at work, rather than the first stirrings of an interest in fashion. Ralph chose clothes not because they were "in" but for what they could do for him and his ego. He loved it when he found something like an old army surplus parka because the way he wore it always elicited the response

Above left: Ralph with his brother Jerry.
Above right: Ralph and Ricky on Lake Como, 1969.

"And you couldn't copy his look. You could try but you wouldn't look the way he did. He was never the group's shrinking violet."

he wanted from his peer group. "That's cool," "Where did you get that?" and, most rewarding of all, "Where can I get it?" Those were the kind of reactions that showed you were liked. Not that being liked was a problem for Ralph. Although quiet and at times even introspective, he was always popular, as good sportsmen usually are.

Left: The young couple, Ralph and Ricky in East Hampton, 1976.

Contemporaries recall how personal appearance became almost an obsession for Ralph, taking the place of the school studies that so singularly failed to engage his imagination. But it brought its reward. By the time he was sixteen, Ralph Lauren was well established with his neighborhood peer groups as a "dresser." Steve Bell finds his obsession and the reaction interesting. As he says, "We weren't the kind of community where our life was fashion. Our life was sport. How you dressed was never a focal point. We all went to the schoolyard in sneakers, dungarees, and a T-shirt. We didn't spend money on clothes. Ralph would show up in things that were "off the wall" but always looked great. When his brother Lenny came back from service in Korea, Ralph started to wear his army clothes—the ponchos and fatigues. It was a great look on him. His father wore old-fashioned striped shirts with white collars—and Ralph started to wear these as well. You could try to copy his look but you wouldn't look the way he did. He was never the group's shrinking violet."

"You have to remember Ralph was very popular," Bell claims. "We just played ball all the time—in the schoolyard or down on the parkway—and he was good at that and he had a great sense of humor. We talked and laughed a lot—if we weren't in the movies or looking for girls. He and I were both very young when we had our first girlfriends."

Ralph was always image-conscious. Bell recalls an escapade that landed him and Ralph in serious trouble, although their actions were motivated by the highest intentions. When they were no older than ten or eleven, they had a school contemporary who, as Bell puts it, was a terrible nerd with shockingly unruly hair. Bell remembers, "None of the girls would go near him and Ralph, who even then was an exceptionally kind person, said, 'Look, guys, we've gotta do something for him.' He was scruffy, the butt of jokes, and Ralph was really sorry for him. We were all in my apartment one afternoon and Ralph decided this poor guy would look better with his hair cut. So he went to the kitchen, came back with some scissors and did just that. Ralph was sure that he wouldn't just look better with a receding hairline, he would look cool—which is what we all wanted, in those days. He really thought he was making this guy look good, but we got into such trouble when his mother came and told my mother. Of course, we were only kids but, interestingly enough, when Ralph was in his late teens and under the influence of Cary Grant or whoever, he decided it would be sexy if he had a receding hairline. He shaved his hair back to create the effect. But that was Ralph, always focused on a physical look which made him feel good."

By the time Ralph finished high school, he knew that his dreams of being an athlete would not be realized. Even in those days, there was a strongly practical streak in him which made acceptance easier. The same practical streak helped him accept that the family's Russian name—Lifshitz—did not easily translate into an English idiom. It never quite sounded right as an American surname. When Ralph was in his teens, Jerry decided to change his name. Leonard did the same. The new name was Lauren and Ralph had no difficulty with taking it as his surname also. His parents retained their Russian name. Nobody quite recalls how the name Lauren came to be chosen but it was a perfect choice. Easily pronounced and remembered, classless and entirely American, it fitted the Lauren brothers and their aspirations like a glove. Although definitely not inspired by the actress Lauren Bacall, she had already made it a fashionable name, well known across America and the world. There were others changes in Ralph's life at this time. Just as a new surname represented a refocussing there were other decisions to be made. His parents had accepted that he was not Rabbi material—although his mother had especially hoped he might be when he was younger—and Ralph knew that following a profession such as law, teaching or medicine was not for him. Moving towards a career of his own choice, he enrolled at the City of New York in order to study business management.

Exposure to films, girls, and the New York environment had taught Ralph many things about himself but one of the most seminal experiences in his life occurred when he was seventeen and, again following Jerry, went for the first time to summer camp at Camp Roosevelt in the Catskills, as a waiter. Jerry says it was part of the process of his brother coming into his own. "He got kind of more handsome," he says, "and that gave him a lot of confidence. He got rid of the baby face. One of the things which happened was that the difference in our ages seemed to shrink. We were very close. We seemed to do everything in step and Camp Roosevelt was no different. In fact, Lenny was the first to go there. We all became camp counsellors, which means you are in charge of a group of kids. You teach them athletics and how to coexist." And, if you came from the Bronx, you also learned. For Ralph, this was his first full experience of people from different backgrounds from his own. Most of the pupils at Camp Roosevelt were from well-off middle-class backgrounds and Ralph found their attitudes, confidence, and dress patterns interesting and informative. In a way, they were confirmation of things that had already begun to stir within himself.

Camp Roosevelt was a seminal experience for Ralph Lauren. The three summers in which he worked there were not only a social epiphany, they also had a great effect on his confidence. His achievements were considerable. He moved from being a waiter to the much more important job of color counsellor, for which he was chosen because he was exceedingly popular. As he says, "We had these things called color wars. The kids would be divided into groups, each with a different color, for example red, blue and green, so that they could be recognized and bond with each other. For everything they did—sports, shows, singing—points were awarded. It was very competitive and the color counsellor's job was to inspire his teams so that they came out top. I loved the spirit, and loved the competition. There was a girls' general and a boys' general, and to be chosen for either was a great honor. It was a recognition, and being made the boys' general when I was about nineteen at that point was probably the biggest thing in my life. I was proud because I'd come from nowhere and I had worked my way up each summer until I became the top counsellor. OK, you can say it was nothing when you look at the rest of my career, but all I know is that, at the time, it was very important to me. Very important."

What Camp Roosevelt did for Ralph was to change the ersatz into the real. Much of the confidence he had portrayed when a younger teenager had been bravado, but after the summer camps Ralph had grown into a man. His confidence now came from self-knowledge—the knowledge of who he was and who he could be. In his final yearbook at De Witt Clinton School in 1957, whereas his fellow pupils followed tradition and specified the professions, Ralph Lauren felt sufficiently confident to upset that tradition by writing beneath his picture not a profession but the status to which he aspired. It took only one word. He wrote "millionaire."

Ralph's time at City College was hardly more enjoyable than his time at high school. Although the courses were tailored to his needs much more than were any at De Witt Clinton, it was hard. Studying part-time, often in the evenings, traveling for over an hour each way from the Bronx to Lexington and 23rd, it was a long way from the preppy dreams that Camp Roosevelt had stimulated. He stuck the course for two years before finally dropping out. He was twenty and waiting for the draft: nobody would give him a job. While he was waiting to be drafted, he took part-time posts. During his last years at school and during his time at City College, he had done various jobs, including one at Allied Stores where he had to log returned merchandise. He had champed at the futility of it all, only continuing because the $50 salary had gone toward creating a wardrobe as unique and idiosyncratic as the clothes he used to put together in his early teens. It was all part of his stretching out toward a lifestyle that the times and his background said he could not have—except that, as Steve Bell recalls, "Ralph used to say, 'I'm going to get it! That's what I'm shooting for!' And, of course, he did."

But before that there was the draft. It seems inevitable that while he waited, he should get a temporary job in the men's apparel business. He and Jerry decided to go to Fifth Avenue and visit the Valhalla of old-money, quasi-English gentlemen's dress: Brooks Brothers. Jerry recalls walking through the door. "I thought it was like Mecca," he says. "It was just, 'Wow!'" For Ralph it was the Ivy League altar. Although he didn't know it at the time, Abraham Lincoln, the Duke of Windsor, and F. Scott Fitzgerald, along with every American who wished to dress like a gentleman, had walked through the Brooks Brothers' door. Ralph was delighted when he managed to get a job there whilst he waited for his draft card. It was more exposure to the middle-class approach to dressing. He watched and learned.

Above: Ralph and Ricky at Lime Rock, 1979.

When he finally went into the army, it was with many things to think about, things which Brooks Brothers had brought to his attention. His days in the Reserves were largely spent at Fort Dix. Discharged, due to an injury to his leg, he knew he had to find a job and there seemed only one possible career: gentlemen's clothing. He had learned from Brooks Brothers and the upmarket menswear retailer Paul Stuart, from whom even as a student at City College he had managed to buy clothes; he had spent hours talking with salesmen, not about fashion *per se*, but about the mysteries of clothes, class and style. As a result, he knew there was only one path to take, even though it was a humble one. Ralph Lauren's first full-time, permanent job was packing gloves for the middle-market gloves firm Meyers Make Inc. He still remembers his days in the packing room. "My job was to take the order books of the salesmen, check the number of orders and when they were to be shipped, and then mail them." It bored him almost instantly but he did not quit. Instead, he asked to be given the chance to join the sales force. He got it, but the job was no glamorous sinecure. He was on the lowest level of salesmanship, trying to get orders from budget-conscious store buyers who came to New York to buy the line for their stores across the US. It was hard to get them to see a salesman they didn't know and it was harder to persuade them to write a decent-sized order but Ralph persisted, dashing around with his box of samples, waiting for hours in order to see someone, smiling when his merchandise was dismissed. It was a marvelous proving ground for his talent. He learned the psychology of salesmanship, the nuances of taste and, above all, the art of gentle persuasion.

Above: Ralph and Ricky leaving to attend the Coty Awards, 1977.

Perhaps the most important thing that Ralph had at this stage was his personality. He was assured, but not bombastic; he could talk to all manner of men and make them listen; he smiled easily; he was relaxed. He was perceived by colleagues as essentially a man's man and buyers often ordered simply because they liked his style and were amused—and secretly rather impressed—by his immaculate appearance. Above all, he radiated an enthusiasm for his product that he was far from feeling. As he had known when he first took the job with Meyers Make, gloves could only be a brief stepping-stone to his higher ambitions. On January 23, 1964, he took the next step. He was 25 when he became the New York salesman for the Boston-based tie manufacturer Rivetz. Immediately, he began to cultivate his appearance so that he would always be memorable. He was determined that whenever his name was mentioned there would be no blank looks and nobody would ask, "Who?"

To say that Ralph Lauren was showcasing himself tells only part of the story. He was window-dressing an attitude of mind. It was not in a spirit of pretence that he dressed like no other salesman in the United States. He dressed that way because it was how he believed the role should be costumed. The choices he made every morning—jodhpurs or cords, nipped waist or double-breasted jacket—were a reflection of the part he wished to play. All his life Ralph Lauren has been an actor manqué, dressing for different roles as if his whole existence were a repertory season in which an actor plays many parts and dons many costumes. His first part was as a pert tie salesman. With the brio expected of a good performer, he took care of the props even before the persona began. Because virtually no young man in his world wore a beard, he grew one; because tie salesmen were expected to drive sensible, low-cost, low-profile cars, he drove around New York in an open-topped cream Morgan, with his box of samples on the passenger seat next to him.

Ralph Lauren's easy self-projection was in fact the result of years of observation. The boastful mental skirmishes at the rail had taught him how to capture and control an audience. The hours spent at the movies, involuntarily absorbing every movement of the great stylish stars—Carey Grant, James Stewart and Alan Ladd—Ralph Lauren learned a little from them all. Camp Roosevelt had shown him how the socially secure move, unself-conscious and unaware of how they command their space. Brooks Brothers had taught him how men who are used to having their views go unchallenged use voice and gesture to command attention. They all resulted in a man in his twenties who was consummately in control of his image.

If Camp Roosevelt and Brooks Brothers had their influence on Ralph Lauren and how he was beginning to see himself in the world, his meeting with a young Jewish girl of Austrian descent was to be of even greater significance. Ricky Low-beer, born on January 21, 1945, came from a background rather different from Ralph's. Her parents had been forced to flee Vienna when Hitler came to power in Germany. They went to Shanghai, where they lived for almost a year, before they were able to emigrate to the United States. Her father was the maitre d' and briefly became a singer, entertaining the guests. Unlike Ralph's parents, they were not orthodox although Ricky now sees that both families had many similarities.

"Our backgrounds were very different," she says. "I was an only child, Ralph was one of four. I was protected from the realities of life—such as having to think about money; Ralph was always worldly, even beyond his years, because he learned so much from his brothers. His parents clung to their Jewishness, my family was much more linked to their Europeanism. They were very Viennese. But what they all had in common was that they were very basic people."

Ralph met Ricky by chance. She was a student of Hunter College, studying English, and she worked at an eye doctor's office in order to make some extra money. Ralph needed to visit the eye doctor and on the afternoon he arrived it just happened that the part-time secretary there was Ricky. "He asked me if I would go out with him," she reminisces. "I was very reserved about it. But he was very persistent, so I agreed." He picked me up in his car and I seem to remember I spent most of the time reciting from Chaucer and other poets to him. I'm sure it wasn't what Ralph was expecting." One of Ralph's close friends from the time recalls, "they hit it off immediately. It was obvious Ralph knew that Ricky was something special, even from that first date."

Blonde, with an air of European class, clearly better educated than Ralph, Ricky was the "ideal girl" for whom he had been subconsciously yearning. Looking back, she confesses, "I was sweet, quiet, but with a certain edge. I know I felt very European-American at that time. I was only nineteen and my thinking was still very influenced by my parents. Ralph was totally American-American." She was able to demonstrate that certain edge on their second date. If Ralph thought of her as too academic, she had a surprise for him. He took her dancing and, to his amazed delight, Ricky's unexpected side came out. She says, "Another part-time job I had was teaching dance at the Fred Astaire Dance Studio and I really could dance. So, rather than recite Chaucer… We had so much fun. He got to know what I was like in a more rounded way and I began to see that he was special. He was very, very different from the college boys I had been dating. Much more grown up. He had found a career and taken on its responsibilities. He was working. He even looked different from the other boys I'd known because he dressed totally differently. He actually dressed like my relatives who were all European. He would come to my house on a Sunday in a suit, with a beautiful Macclesfield silk tie, when other young American men would be wearing leisure clothing."

Both Ralph and Ricky remember two important moments in their courtship, which lasted only a brief eight months before they married. The thing that convinced Ricky of the rightness of Ralph happened very early in their courtship. "I was a very good girl," she points out. "I would always come home from a date when I said I would but on this occasion we were having such a good time that we were late. When we got home, Ralph came upstairs to bring me to the door. My mother was furious with me. Really, really angry. I wasn't even that late, maybe half an hour. She was so angry that all Ralph did was to say goodnight and leave. Next day at work I dreaded going home, thinking that when I got home my parents wouldn't speak to me or they'd raise their voices, they were so upset. Finally I got home. My parents came to the door and when they looked at me they were smiling, and I couldn't imagine why. My mother said, 'Do you know who was here?' I said, 'What do you mean?' and she said, 'Ralph was here for breakfast. He came to apologize. He sat with us, he had breakfast,' and he said he hoped that he hadn't upset them too much, that if he had known he would never have kept me out so long and he just hoped that that didn't spoil the chances of them allowing him to continue to date me. Now, nobody I knew ever was brave enough to do that. We had only been going out for a very short time. There was so much character that I saw it made me think yes, he's different from most people. It wasn't about the pinstriped suit this time and it wasn't about the Morgan and it wasn't about the fact that he dressed like the relatives that I'd known; this time it was the character that I recognized and related to."

Ricky also remembers how she passed the test with Ralph. "We would walk down the street, looking in the store windows like everybody seemed to do, you know, just having a casual stroll

"It was obvious Ralph knew that Ricky was something special,
even from that first date."

and I remember once we came up to a store that displayed jean jackets in the windows. We both went in and he said 'Which jacket do you like the best?' and there was a Lee and a Levi and a Wrangler and I commented on which one I liked best and why. He said, 'You know, you really have a good eye. You really get the difference about the stitches and the grommets and this and that,' and, you know it was a test I think. I wonder what would have happened if I hadn't chosen the right jacket!"

Ralph was a member of a family, the center of which was, in Ricky's opinion, his mother. She was the person who set the tone. Ricky was introduced into this world very early on, after only a few dates. She remembers that the apartment was small and decorated with stenciling where Ralph's father had practiced and experimented with different techniques that he could use in his trade. She recalls that there was a samovar and a vitrine with prized pieces of china on display: "… small treasures of a lifetime."

Evidence of Frank Lifshitz's passion flooded the apartment. His love of art was everywhere. "All the tables were painted with flowers or bunches of grapes and all the pictures on the walls were his, copied from art books … an aristocratic Medici-type woman … or pastoral pieces reminiscent of European landscapes—little waterways, canals, cottages. He loved painting." Ralph's mother's passion was food. "Whenever you went there was the smell of food," Ricky remembers. "Eating was terribly important to Ralph's mother. She was always brewing or cooking something."

Frieda was the center point of a busy world. It had been that way since Ralph was a baby. Ricky feels that although it gave him a sense of security, there was a great deal of traffic in that small apartment. "Even when he was a baby," she says, "he saw a lot of movement and gesture around him. There was the food. Above all, there was the conversation. It was always intense, almost urgent. So I think that he was looking around in awe and amazement and wondering what his role would be in that environment someday. He would probably see his brothers running in and out with baseball bats and cameras and they were the cool, young, new Americans. They wanted to know everything and do everything, be everything. They were sports-conscious, they were playing basketball, they were buying cars and he was watching this, watching that as the youngest one, just absorbing everything."

Ralph and Ricky were very much in love and Ralph decided that it was time they married. He found a tiny apartment in Manhattan and put down a deposit. The landlord reneged on the agreement, refused to return the money and, when Ralph took him to arbitration, won on a technicality. When Ralph and Ricky were married on December 20, 1964, they were nearly penniless. But they did have a home. They had found a two-roomed apartment in the Bronx, very near Ralph's parents. Ralph was working for Rivetz and Ricky was finishing her last year of college before she became an elementary school teacher. They had prospects and they had hopes.

Left: The young entrepeneur on the edge of success.

founding an empire

Ralph was becoming increasingly absorbed by all aspects of men's dress. He was already patronizing some of New York's best tailors, men of skill who knew how to blend the avant garde and the traditional to create formal clothes that were elegant and relaxed. Contact with such craftsmen had an enormous effect on Ralph Lauren. Not worrying that a bespoke tailor has to please only one man—the individual customer—he began to speculate as to how original fashion thinking—even design—could be introduced into ties. Hard to imagine now, but to even think of such a possibility in the late sixties in the US was considered not only revolutionary but even subversive, although those in the know, including Ralph, were well aware that it had already been done—and to great success—elsewhere. Menswear was dragging its feet in the US, with most lines being designed anonymously by means of adapting, modifying or refabricating lines that had already proved successful in the previous season. In Europe, however, menswear had become "designer." London was bristling with boutiques specifically aimed at young men—the first time in history that shops had taken over the world of the exclusive Savile Row tailors into whose premises women entered only as adjuncts to their husbands. The Beatles, The Kinks, The Rolling Stones all sang about—and were living demonstrations of—the peacock revolution. In a rainbow burst of colors and textures not seen on the bodies of the male sex for over two hundred years, the man as fashion object was launched. Designers like Hardy Amies, John Stevens, Mr. Fish and the Frenchman Pierre Cardin were there to meet the new sartorial needs stimulated by pop music and new menswear magazines aimed at the young.

Daily News Rec

the big knot

Above: Press coverage for the new ties was instant and enthusiastic.

In the middle of all the extrovert drama, the kipper tie, up to four inches wide at its fullest point, became an outstanding feature of the new look. It was as far removed from traditional neckwear as it possibly could be. Velvet, satin, needlepoint, tapestry, and cord were used to produce ties in a kaleidoscope of patterns, textures and colors. They were worn by the avant-garde in Europe, however Ralph Lauren was working in the New York tie business and that was a very different story. His approach was both more commercial and more realistically creative. His ties, every bit as revolutionary as those appearing in London, were not to be flamboyantly flashy fashion statements to be photographed around the neck of a rock star and then forgotten. They were conceived as a serious new fashion direction, something to appeal to a wide range of American men.

His first attempts to bring a degree of modernity into the traditional world of tie manufacture were not successful but his winning ways and persuasive tongue broke down resistance sufficiently for him to introduce a very modest degree of innovation. But it tended to stop there. His close friend and colleague, Joe Barato, who had first met him when they both worked at Brooks Brothers, remembers the early struggles and Ralph's determination not to deviate from a level of perfection he had set for himself. "It was just the way he always was, right from the first day I met him at Brooks Brothers," he recalls. "I remember looking into a showcase at a tie display. I'd never seen ties so beautifully assorted. They were so impeccable, they looked like soldiers. I asked who'd done them and, of course, it was Ralph. We became close friends and when we left to go to different jobs we kept in touch. When he worked at Rivetz we would have lunch almost weekly. He always talked about his plans. He knew that the US market could stand wide ties and yet he couldn't make his bosses understand." It was the bosses who were out of step. In one of those synergies of creative energy which happen in fashion whereby two sensibilities evolve a new style (as with Mary Quant and Andre Courrege with the birth of the mini) Ralph Lauren was simultaneously creating the wide tie as a new fashion direction.

Marvin Traub, at that time president and eventually to become chairman of Bloomingdale's, takes up the story in his book *Like No Other Store…*, "Ralph yearned to apply some of his personal style to the necktie field." It was style which had already earned him a place in *Daily News Record* (*DNR*), the Fairchild Publications trade newspaper for menswear, in an article praising his dress sense and style. But Rivetz were as traditional as the rest of the tie trade and they had no faith in the idea that Ralph—a maverick if not a total eccentric in their opinion—could carry through his dreams. As Traub says, "At the time, ties were dark and narrow. Ralph had an idea for a wide tie that he wanted Rivetz to carry." They refused. He began to look around in the hope of finding a firm that would agree. His break came when the highly successful Cincinnati-based firm of Beau Brummell took him on. Not that president Ned Brower was about to give him carte blanche. But Ralph's persuasive skills did seduce Brower into agreeing to start a small new division, which Ralph would run, just to see if there could be a market for the sort of ties he talked of so enthusiastically. They would be wide—up to four inches across. Most American ties were two to three inches wide. They would be exotic in color and fabric. Above all, they would be expensive. In a market with a price range from $2.00 to $5.00; Ralph planned to have his start at $7.50 and rise to an unheard of $15.00.

His division was a one-man band. He did everything himself. He designed the ties, supervised their manufacture, packed and distributed them, and, above all, he sold them. It was all done from a desk in a tiny showroom in the Empire State Building. But nothing about the labels sewn in the back of each tie suggested anything so humble.

Many claim to have witnessed the birth of Polo—and even to have acted as midwife to the idea. It has been suggested that Jerry Lauren first thought of the name. But Joe Barato recalls Ralph frequently sketching a man on a horse and then coming up with the name once he had an embryonic logo in his head. "He called me," Barato says. "He said, 'Joe. I got a name.' 'What is it?' I said. 'What is it? Polo.' All I could say was 'perfect.' In fact, his first business cards didn't even have his name on. Just that word. Guys thought they had an appointment to see Mr. Polo." Barrato was right. Polo was the perfect name for the sort of distinction Ralph Lauren intended his product to have. It was a little pretentious, a little snobby—and completely memorable. Ralph says that he tried many names with associations with sport but none of them had the connotations of class that Polo brings. Even today, 35 years after the event, Polo still has the resonance of polo the game. Played by the established wealthy such as Prince Charles, the fact that it is an upper-class game which requires strings of ponies does nothing to exclude the nouveau riche, from rock stars to the sons of Argentinian cattle barons. But it is not only associations of money, position, and breeding that the word Polo carries. Like the game, it is a celebration of masculinity. Once dismissed as croquet on four legs, the image could not be further from the truth. Polo is a demanding, even frightening game, requiring courage, fitness, and fast reactions—all the things admired by a sportsman like Lauren.

The name was a masterstroke. All Ralph had to do now was learn the business. In this, he was lucky in his choice of wife: Ricky's father had worked in the tie business himself for over seventeen years, along with a friend, Sydney Horowitz, who had also been in the trade many years. Ricky had known Sydney all her life and she was delighted when her father, only too aware of the pitfalls facing a relative newcomer in any branch of the garment business, suggested to Ralph that he should have Sydney advise him. As a result, Sydney's sons Joel and Alan, who is currently vice-chairman of Tommy Hilfiger, also joined Ralph's staff.

Ralph was searching around for markets and finding that the traditions of the tie business were not so easily cast aside. Top-class tailors understood what he was trying to do, several of his fellows in the business found themselves increasingly liking his ties, but retailers were nervous. Bloomingdale's agreed to take a token number, on two conditions: that they were made more narrow and that they carried the Bloomingdale's label. Ralph rejected both suggestions, not through unbending arrogance but in realization that they would make his ties like all others on sale in Bloomingdale's. He knew from what was happening in Europe as well as from the reaction from professionals that his day would come. If he watered down his concept, he would be discredited. But in all the uncertainties, he had in Ricky not just a support but a "rock." She recalls, "when he went on his own I wrote him a letter telling him I would never fear for us because I believed in him and knew that, whatever he wanted to do, he would be able to do it. I remember writing, 'I know you have the feeling you can fly. I know you can, and I want you to fly.'"

Nevertheless, it took Ralph Lauren over a year to make any real headway. He managed to get his ties featured in *Playboy* and he was interviewed by *DNR*. But things were moving slowly enough that many would have seen it as pure fantasy when he told *DNR* "My long-range wish

Polo was the perfect name for the sort of distinction Ralph Lauren intended his product to have.

would be to design all kinds of menswear, not just ties." Progress was slow, but there was some progress. More Polo ties were seen every day, around the necks of reps and people in the trade. Bloomingdale's had given in and were not just stocking but selling Ralph's wide ties at high prices.

The change in attitude had partly been brought about by a persistent guerrilla campaign on Ralph's behalf by fellow tie salesman Joe Aezen who, although he worked for a different company, pushed Ralph's ties every time he visited Bloomingdale's. It paid off. Marvin Traub remembers Ralph being "ecstatic" at the change of heart. "And," he adds, "he was not going to leave anything to chance. He delivered the ties himself and would call in at least twice a week to see that they were being displayed the way he wanted. On Saturday mornings, he would arrive early to restock his showcase. He was a colorful character, pulling up outside the store in his sports car and wearing jeans and a bomber jacket. He even demonstrated to the sales force exactly how his ties must be tied, with a little dimple below the knot, just so." It was, Traub now believes, the very beginning of the explosion in American's menswear that finally routed the prejudice surrounding designer fashion for men. Already, Lauren was being wooed by a New Jersey-based suitmaker called Norman Hilton, who wanted him to make ties to match his suits. Tempting as it was, Ralph declined. He was so totally wedded to his dream of being in business for himself that he could not imagine compromising his vision by partnerships. In 1968 Ralph formed his own company, Polo Fashions Inc. The label in the garments read "Polo by Ralph Lauren." It was a label the fashion industry was now taking very seriously. Most crucially, what Ralph was doing was supported by the menswear trade publication *Daily News Record* (DNR), the undisputed arbiter. Its feisty young fashion editor, Buffy Birritella, totally believed in Ralph Lauren's revolutionary approach to menswear. She wrote about him extensively in major stories featured his clothes on the cover, and generally raised awareness of what he was doing. It was no surprise when, in 1970, he received the coveted Coty Award for menswear, clear proof that he had established his own fashion field, reinforced two years later when he was given the Menswear Return Award.

As the sixties slid into the seventies, Ralph Lauren was eager to expand his business. Since beginning to produce his own line of ties in 1967, he had come to share the frustration felt by his wife Ricky at not being able to find the clothes she wanted—clothes that were the equivalent of her husband's menswear. "We used to spend Saturdays doing all the stores," Ralph recalls, "and we nearly always ended up depressed and frustrated because there was nothing that we wanted to buy."

Fashion was in transition. Like every other city in the world, New York looked to London for its fashion culture. The simple and direct approach exemplified by David Bailey and Jean Shrimpton was being edged aside. Fashion was looking for something different, something more complex. It wanted less girl-next-door and more exoticism, less Twiggy and more Verushka. This was true not merely in New York boutiques like Abracadabra and Paraphernalia which, against a background of Indian wall hangings and oriental brass, offered an experience that was not so much a fashion as a cultural adventure, but equally in the big stores. Fashion was on an "anything-goes" spree that excited the media but, in fact, interested only the most trend-conscious: a minute slice of the overall marketing cake across North America, where department stores and boutiques were looking for something with the widest possible appeal, something with which a broad spectrum of the US buying public could identify.

In response, American fashion finally began to rid itself of the creative cringe that had previously characterized its attitude to French fashion. Since the thirties, top American stores had looked to Paris for inspiration each season, following the trends shown there and adapting them for the top end of sophisticated ready-to-wear. Seventh Avenue also based its business on Paris, offering watered-down, more accessible versions of the Paris look at popular prices. But indigenous American design, generically described as sportswear, had long been an important element in the American woman's wardrobe and had produced designers of talent and vision: In the forties Claire McCardell, Sydney Wragge, and Clare Potter barely glanced at Paris. Their approach to design was based on what American women needed in order to live American lives. They spearheaded a strong movement which, in the hands of Lauren, Perry Ellis, and Calvin Klein, was destined to exert a world influence equal to, if not greater than, that of Paris in terms of real clothes which women would actually buy and wear. The transition from the old order coincided perfectly with Ralph Lauren's decision to dip a toe into the lucrative women's market in response to the urging of many of his admirers and supporters. The omens for such a move were good: The grand old New York fashion firms such as Hattie Carnegie and Lily Daché, who had always relied on Paris to give a lead, were gone; department stores were closing their millinery and couture departments in favor of boutiques designed to compete with what was happening in the many independent little shops in city areas not normally associated with fashion. Greenwich Village and the cross streets between Third and Sixth Avenues were attracting more young people than the traditional fashion stores on Fifth and Lexington. The legendary retail genius, Geraldine Stutz, was revitalizing Henri Bendel, making it the place in which young designers longed to have their work displayed.

By early June 1971, Polo had managed to take a hold in the womanswear business, albeit a modest one. In response to increasing pleas from customers and retailers for a woman's blouse that would replicate the quality and class of his men's shirt range, Ralph had decided to produce an equivalent for women—but it was to be a shirt, not a blouse. As Jeffrey Banks, one of Ralph Lauren's early assistants in womenswear, recalls, "Ralph had fallen in love with Cacharel shirts and he bought them for Ricky. She's tiny—size two—and everything was done with her in mind. His whole reason for going into women's wear was clothing for his wife." In this Banks is right, of course. Ralph Lauren's ambition, always strong, had been given an enormous shot in the arm by the success of his menswear. But he knew that no matter how much interest it might continue to attract, men's fashion was limited. It could only achieve a certain amount of publicity and fame. He also knew that this situation was unlikely to change. Men's fashion was a victim of the male psyche. Women talk to each other about clothes, men do not—and Ralph Lauren knew that his career was at a point where he needed talk. That meant women's clothes and Seventh Avenue. If he was nervous of the former, he was deeply suspicious of the latter, feeling that traditional American rag-trade attitudes were not in tune with his thinking. Nevertheless, he bit the bullet, not only because it was inevitable but also because he could see the first faint glimmer of a future that would transcend even his most ambitious dreams. And yes, it would please him to dress Ricky in the way he felt a modern woman should be clothed. He would start with blouses seeing how they could be made more American, fresher, more … Ralph Lauren. They would be done absolutely

with Ricky in mind. Banks amply recalls the first shirts, both their beauty and their problems: "He made beautiful candy stripes with white collars and cuffs, Ascot shirts, paisleys, and so forth."

Buffy Birrittella, at the time Lauren's publicist and assistant and currently executive vice president of women's design and advertising, was an early recruit to the business, also remembers those first forays into womenswear as a part of Ralph's developing philosophy of dress. "Ralph's womenswear was about style, quality, and a look of self-assurance. Mind you, the cut was very skinny. I tried something on from those early years just recently and I couldn't bend my arm! Everything was fitted on me and I was very slight in those days. It was a very trim fit. But that's what Ralph wanted. The fit had to be very precise, tight to the body and very feminine."

"Ralph didn't want bust darts," Banks explains. "He wanted the shirts to look like a man's shirt, very fitted, very high under the arms. So, if you were normally size eight, you had to buy size ten or twelve. We ended up having to make sixteens and eighteens because women couldn't get into the shirts. Not only that, if they had a bust, the front would pull open. The strange thing was that it became a status symbol to be able to fit into them. Women still wanted them and, when we corrected the sizing problem, they sold."

Marvin Traub finds a different reason for the success of Lauren's women's shirts, despite their high, tight armholes. As loyal and generous with Ralph's womenswear as he had been for his menswear, Lauren had done what he has done throughout his career, as Traub points out. "He found a gap in the market. There was already a large business in women's blouses in the early seventies. You have only to think of Anne Klein, the most important sportswear designer at that time. But her appeal was to the fashion-conscious woman who was looking for something very feminine and soft. Ralph was thinking of what his wife and other women of her generation were wanting to wear."

Man-tailored shirts did not exist as a female fashion item. As Traub points out, "He was moving in a new direction. In fact, he'd uncovered a new retailing opportunity. But—and this is the cleverness of Ralph Lauren—he presented his new line in a way that gave it instant cachet. On the shirt cuff he placed a polo player—for, as he said, 'that little touch, like a piece of jewellery'—and the label read 'Polo by Ralph Lauren.'" Both were masterstrokes because they removed the Lauren product from the arena of women's blouses and, at a time when career women were wishing to dress with the same authority as men, gave them by association a link with his menswear. Above all, by using his own name he had identified himself as a designer rather than merely another womenswear brand.

Traub gave Ralph a space for his shirts in Bloomingdale's. "It was on the top of the escalator on the third floor," Banks recalls. "It was just a little shirt bar but everybody saw it from the escalator." It was an instant success. Despite the fact that they were appreciably more expensive than anything similar in the store, Bloomingdale's immediately sold out of the first shirts. It was not surprising: the seductive ad-speak created for a special promotion contained all the right buzz-words for the time. "And now," the copy read, "Polo by Ralph Lauren for the girls. The most liberated shirt in town—it's that fabulous man's world shirt… assured stripes, thoroughbred solids… collared and cuffed in white… all wearing the symbolic polo player on the cuff. Polo, in well-bred cotton, 6–16, $24." It was archetypal Polo Ralph Lauren speak, inviting women into a world of relaxed, socially assured elegance, backed by associations with the authority of men's tailoring and the breeding found in the top echelons of American society. With such connections, the shirts were bound to sell.

Left: The Ralph Lauren ideal—the perfect couple and their dogs in the country.

Early menswear advertising imagery.

Bloomingdale's were delighted. They had taken a risk but the results were a triumphant vindication. Marvin Traub wondered what could come next with Ralph Lauren, to their mutual benefit. To the question, "What else do you want to do?" Ralph replied, after a little thought, that he felt the moment was right for him to produce a full womenswear line. Traub agreed that it was the next logical move. As he wrote in *Like No Other Store*, he was sure on the evidence so far that "Women might talk about Kenzo but they were going to wear Ralph Lauren." He could even accept that because Ralph wanted his clothes to have what Buffy called "that skinny European fit," his customers would have to be prepared to "size up." The experience with the shirts had made it clear that if the merchandise was desirable enough, size would be only a minor consideration. Traub's store buyers would have liked the cut to be modified to make fitting easier for women but, as Buffy says, "It was the look. We knew they didn't fit everybody. But that was part of the thing. We did adjust the fit, but only very slightly. We needed to retain the fashion look of the shirts. What Ralph was doing was an instant hit with the customers although a lot of the press didn't 'get it.' In fact, it was never about fashion even though it became a fashion to wear skinny shirts and tailored clothing. It was so contrary to what was going on in women's clothing. I mean, Yves Saint Laurent was doing hippy, gypsy-peasant, everything was loose and easy, and we were so tailored. I am sure that not everyone understood."

But enough did. And they were keen to buy, even though Ralph Lauren was producing the most expensive sportswear on the market, way beyond the price point of Anne Klein and even Bill Blass. However, the popularity of Ralph's womenswear immediately raised a problem. He barely had the staff to branch out so quickly into other fields: less than ten months after his initial foray into shirts, Bloomingdale's built a womenswear department for him, to stand on the third floor alongside the European big names of the time, including Yves Saint Laurent, Sonia Rykiel, and Missoni. This was the second of his shops in the store, the first being his own name menswear boutique. As the only American designer to receive this accolade, he pioneered the 'shop in shop' concept. To put him in with famous, international names and give him a selling space equal to that of Saint Laurent was, as Traub admits, a risk—but it was also a great compliment and vote of confidence which Ralph really appreciated. "Although I knew I belonged there," he says, "and I knew I'd sell I also knew that other retailers were watching, waiting to see what would happen."

Ralph, Buffy, and Sal Cesarini—a sketcher who understood pattern-making and had a tailoring background, brought in to supply desperately needed technical knowledge and to record the ideas—worked on the designs together. Buffy well recalls those early designing days. "We would pick out the fabrics with Ralph. It would always start with the fabrics. When we were working on menswear, we would work on womenswear in terms of the fabrics. Even though it's a shirt for men, the fabric would make a great little tailored shirtwaist dress. Sal would be sketching, taking down the ideas, and then Ralph and I would look at it and go, 'No, the lapel's too big,' or 'It needs three buttons; it's too long; it needs to be shorter.' We would take the details from our men's pants and make them into skirts. It was always about a 'non-fashion' fashion look so it was always about that kind of contradiction, which has always interested Ralph. It's for someone who doesn't look like she's trying too hard, where it's all coming together and it just seems like a part of her innate style: she's wearing the clothes, the clothes aren't wearing her. She's very confident; she's very comfortable in her clothes, and so nothing is forced or gimmicky or costumey. So right at the beginning a philosophy evolved, even if the reference was menswear. We always asked, 'Okay, so what's the best shirt and what's the fabric? What's the stitching? What does the collar look like? How do you make that exciting for a woman and put the polo player on it?' You know, that doesn't seem like much now but it gave everything that little touch, that little attention to detail. It's like doing leather and doing contrast stitching on it so although it's leather it references the best jean jacket you've ever seen, but done now in beautiful leathers in great colors and that sort of thing. So it never goes out of style. I mean, yes, there are things that go in and out but if it has an integrity and an authenticity and that reference behind it, you always relate to it."

Many people have asked what it is that makes Ralph Lauren unique. There are many answers but the most convincing explanation for what makes him one of the world's most influential designers, able to understand and articulate the aspirations of millions of women, is the philosophy that was the basis of his approach to designing for women even in these early stages. The man who has notoriously claimed that fashion is baloney began as he intended to continue. Ralph Lauren was not creating anti-fashion, as many Belgian and Japanese designers do today. Nor was he creating alternative fashion. What he set out to do and achieved with resounding success was to design clothes that enabled women who were not deeply interested in fashion but who wished their clothes to reflect the elegance and sophistication of their lives to stand next to the fashionably dressed, hold their own, and even, perhaps, make the super-fashionable seem slightly ridiculous. As he says, "My woman can walk into a fashionable gathering in Paris just wearing a simple cashmere twinset, pearls, perfectly cut flannel pants, and loafers, and make the others look insignificant." As he is talking, he is thinking of the great actresses whose appearance has so influenced his visual approach: Katharine Hepburn, Grace Kelly, Lauren Bacall, and Audrey Hepburn—the ones who, on- and off-screen, exuded a relaxed elegance bred from confidence.

What Ralph Lauren proposed was not unique. Chanel had understood the appeal of the *dégagé* approach to dress and had used it in her second coming when she reopened her fashion house in 1954 and showed what became known quite simply as "the Chanel Suit." Before that, the philosophy behind Ralph's idea of female fashion had been current since the early thirties in England, the country that, apart from the United States, has had the most profound and lasting influence on his thinking, specifically, the England of the upper classes: male dominated, country oriented, and largely indifferent to the shallow seasonal shifts of Paris fashion. If, by definition, fashion is an urban-based, cosmopolitan phenomenon, then style is country based and, throughout history, has almost always been male-led. Upper-class English women from the thirties through the fifties used their couturiers to provide them with a female equivalent of what their fathers, brothers, and husbands were wearing. For every ballgown they ordered each season, they required far more suits in country tweed, town tweed, fine worsted, or flannel. They further required impeccable cut, superb workmanship, and virtually no "design." Many of the grandest women in Britain had their country suits cut and "built" by their husband's tailor just as his bootmaker made them sturdy leather brogues suitable for stable and paddock in Gloucestershire but tough enough to withstand moorland bogs in Scotland and Ireland.

It was a world Ralph Lauren instinctively understood, a world that he knew he would find more satisfying and sustaining than the glossy world of high fashion. His instincts told him what to do and how to do it. Furthermore, he knew how to spread the word. He was focussed and

Right: Confidence and elegance
were Lauren trademarks even in
the seventies.

articulate when, occasionally, talking about his vision and he was keen to point out what made him and his women's fashion different from the rest of Seventh Avenue. He delivered the message with passion and self-belief. Even now, 35 years on, conviction and sincerity shine out from the yellowing press clippings: "Status fashion isn't what's in today and out tomorrow… the new status symbols are all about permanence and durability… fashion needs to unburden women of fuss, feathers, and fanfare… the world is full of women who aren't clothes crazy but they're sure as hell interested in style—especially their own."

Lauren's performances, softly spoken and unemphatic, mesmerized the American public, whether he was on television or reported in newspapers and magazines. For the media, he was the dream ticket—Mr. Nice Guy, Joe Normal, he could be sold for exactly what he was, an everyday guy with a vision that lifted him from the ordinary to the unique. Dressed as a Western dude, an English squire, and even a Wall Street banker, he exuded straight masculinity. No limp movements, no swishing butt. He seemed a dress designer almost by stealth or accident. And, of course, there was the voice. Ann Boyd, the British woman who ran the Lauren European empire in the eighties, speaks for many when she says that the way Ralph speaks gives him a unique charm, beguiling to women and disarming for men. She struggles to explain: "It's not exactly a lisp, it's more a slight hesitancy over certain syllables. It makes him immensely attractive to listen to." Whatever it was, it added up to an American gold-standard personality which was, as Ralph was shrewdly aware, extremely bankable. The man was leading the fashion. Customers of both sexes felt they were buying into his beliefs when they purchased his clothes, something they did not necessarily feel when they bought the labels of designers such as Yves Saint Laurent or Missoni. Furthermore, they trusted him to deliver the dream he promised—a uniquely American dream, built on a very American attitude. As Ralph maintains, "I don't know exactly how I got involved with the whole English thing but I did and it was very important to me but, whatever it was, I saw it entirely through American eyes. I was always designing American clothes, for American men and women."

It was this American attitude that first attracted Geraldine Stutz to Lauren's womenswear. Brought in to revitalize Henri Bendel in the early sixties, her career during that and the following decade could be said to run broadly parallel to Ralph's. Renowned as one of the great retail talents of her time, she came to the store having worked at Vogue. She had a sharp fashion intelligence but, when it came to buying established European names, lacked the budget to compete with the bigger stores such as Bergdorf Goodman and Lord & Taylor. To counteract this, she largely eschewed Paris and looked to the movers in London, such as Jean Muir and Mary Quant, while keeping an eye on the beginners in America. "We were the first people to have what became known as 'the street of shops,' that is, boutiques within the store," she claims. To fill these spaces, she looked in her own backyard and one of the talents she spotted was Ralph Lauren. "He was already enjoying great success with his menswear in Bloomingdale's," she says. "So I went to look at his very small womenswear collection in his showroom and I just thought that what he was doing was terrific: fresher and better on all scores than anything the big mass women's sportswear manufacturers were producing. His things had enormous quality and integrity. It wasn't just men's stuff turned into womenswear. I could see right away that he was the dreamer of dreams. And I got his message completely."

Above: Fall 1975.

Stutz remembers how simple it was to set up a business arrangement, compared with the multifaceted contracts required today. "I just said to Ralph, 'Things are just wonderful. Let's present you.' And that was it. I've never run into anyone who had such a clear-cut idea of how he wanted his merchandise to be presented. Luckily, what he wanted was how I saw it as well. He and I did the shop together. We found a marvelous old D-shaped counter someplace—all the counters were green baize-lined—and we had hat boxes stacked on top of the armoires. In spirit it was exactly what Ralph was to do on a much bigger scale when he opened his own store. Our space was very 'specialty,' hardly bigger than a room in a house, but the merchandise just walked out. Ralph and I spent a lot of time going around second-hand places on the West Side, looking for odd things to furnish the space. I remember we bought second-hand rugs at the Central Rug Company. Ralph was very 'take charge' even in those days and one day he decided to change my eyeglasses. I was wearing very big ones at that time and he insisted I change to something smaller, more classic and refined. Not that we were always in agreement. We fought like cat and dog but never about something trivial. Always about a principle. In the end, it all came together—with a very big personal involvement from him. He was such a wildly eager beaver, so passionate not to be moved from his dreams by anything. His strength lies in his determination to stick with what he believes in and to do it exactly in the way he sees it—the clothes, the presentation, the lifestyle."

It was May 1972 when Ralph Lauren showed his first complete women's collection, but he had already discovered that his ability to produce clothes which appealed to a much wider range of men and women than even he could have predicted was outstripping his rudimentary skills as a businessman. Eleven months earlier, in June 1971, when he appeared to be on the crest of a wave, having already twice won a Coty award for his menswear, he had hit a serious cashflow problem. He found himself unable to meet his payroll. He turned for help to the man who had championed him so wholeheartedly from the beginning and had become a friend, despite the difference in their ages. Marvin Traub had not reached the point he had by making wild promises. When Ralph told him he needed $50,000 on advance he merely said, "I'll see what I can do." He went to Larry Lachman, chairman of Bloomingdale's, and outlined Ralph's predicament. As he explains in *Like No Other Store*, "I knew it was unusual, but Ralph was the American designer the store had bet on, and we had to support him. To his credit, Larry agreed immediately."

It was expedient but it did not solve the problem. The financial difficulties continued and Ralph Lauren found himself facing a crisis by 1973. As he explains, "I guess I was doing too much. I was undercapitalized. I ran into some financial tightening." It began to look to outsiders that, despite his amazing success, he could lose everything. He decided to ease the crisis by licensing his womenswear to the Kreisler Group. Chief executive officer Stuart Kreisler was a friend of Ralph's, which seemed to him to make the arrangement less tricky. Both men trusted each other and, in fact, Kreisler was one of the people who had originally encouraged Ralph to go into the women's business. Nevertheless, being highly protective of his name and never having licensed any product before, there was no question: Ralph would continue as designer. Traub explains, "His vision of Polo Ralph Lauren was so strong that he felt that, even under license, only he could maintain the right image and the proper quality, but he had to make the decision: license or go under." Being Ralph Lauren, he licensed but he kept full control of design, quality advertising and marketing.

Above left and right: The laid-back
assurance of the early shows set the
tone for everything that was to come.

Like everyone who is successful on a world scale, Ralph Lauren stands charged with having unwavering dedication, being unable to compromise and unwilling to give way. But success comes from ducking and weaving while always keeping an eye not only on the ball but also on the ultimate goal. He admits that the word "control" features a lot in his conversation, and he makes no apologies. "Of course I've always wished to control my own business," he says. "I believe I've had success with what I do not only because I listen to what people say to me but also because I listen to my own gut feelings. I do only what I personally believe in, even when my friends and associates say, 'Are you kidding? You must be crazy!'" But he admits that, certainly in the early days, he made mistakes along the way. "I've had some really major problems. I've had periods when I thought I'd go out of business," he says, adding that, at the time he had to turn to Traub for help, "I nearly lost everything. I had to put all my savings back into the company and rethink my entire structure. I had to learn to work with licensees but I also learned that sharing control doesn't necessarily mean losing anything. It really means retaining the freedom to say no. And that is very important for me." He came through a steep and hard learning curve but he came through strengthened rather than changed.

Naturally, Ralph Lauren will not bow to counsel he feels is wrong, any more than would any man with a strong and fully formed vision. When creative integrity is involved, the margin of compromise is even smaller. He wished to keep control of every aspect of his business but he already knew that, important as the manufacture of his clothes was, the standards the market required could be achieved most successfully by people who had expertise and experience which, at that point, he lacked. He also knew that his vision of women's fashion was so personal to him that the design could never be farmed out to anybody else. To sign with Kreisler was the lesser of the evils and, in most respects, a small price to pay for stability. Polo Ralph Lauren had grown too big too quickly for Ralph and he needed more money and more staff to further execute his vision and enterprise. As Buffy says, "We were all so hands-on in those days. Ralph, Jerry, Sal Cesarino and I did everything, even going to the factories—just as we do today but now we have more staff to support that fastidiousness."

Lauren had built up a reputation for quality, as *The New York Times* commented on the first full womenswear collection in May 1972: "With all the talk about classics, someone was bound to bring back the mannish tailored suit. Fortunately it was Ralph Lauren, who knows something about tailoring." It was an enviable reputation and Ralph knew that it must be preserved at any cost. There were changes in the air and they had to be addressed. As one of his colleagues explained to journalist Jeffrey A. Trachtenberg, "The thing that set Ralph apart was his singlemindedness of purpose… he wasn't trendy… it's the single most important thing about him. To this day, there are people walking around saying, 'Ralph Lauren isn't that special. I could have done it….' They couldn't be more wrong. Ralph is the most special guy in the apparel business. He had integrity" And that was something Ralph Lauren would not put in jeopardy, no matter how many expedients and compromises might be forced on him. But he could see advantages to his new situation. As he explained in an interview he gave for the Oral History Collection of The Fashion Institute of Technology in 1990, "I couldn't do everything. The beauty of licensing was the ability to expand into new products without choking yourself financially. It

"The thing that set Ralph apart was his single-mindedness of purpose …
he wasn't trendy … it's the single most important thing about him."

gave me the opportunity to say, 'Okay, I can design this womenswear but I can't afford to do it all.
I can't grow a company.' The reason I stayed in business was that I went into retailing and I also
kept control of the advertising."

Perhaps more importantly, he constantly monitored the attitude of his core customer,
exemplified by his wife, Ricky. Whereas he instinctively knew how the particular type of man he
was targeting with his menswear wished to look—hardly surprising, as he was his own template
and sounding board—he needed input about his womenswear. It was something Buffy constantly
gave him in their day-to-day working situation but the reaction that really mattered was that
of his wife. As he explained in an interview in the eighties, "She's the best barometer for me.
Living with a woman gives you a real insight, you get a first-hand knowledge of what a woman
wants; what she needs; what she's tired of. And what she's got too much of. I'm always looking at
what is not around. What my wife doesn't have. What she would like to wear. What I'd like to
see her in."

Ralph Lauren openly expresses his view that he has never been given his full due in fashion
circles, a question addressed elsewhere in this book. Many impartial witnesses to the last 35 years
are inclined to agree. Lauren moved up the fashion ladder with lightning speed. By the second half
of the seventies every major magazine and newspaper were clamoring for him. He made for
perfect stories: young, fit, with cowboy eyes and a relaxed demeanor worthy of Steve McQueen,
one of his great heroes. He photographed well. He talked well. Many found his charm—a mixture
of self-effacement and little-boy bragging—delightfully seductive. Female journalists—and most
fashion journalists were women—were thrilled with what they saw. They were also thrilled with
what they heard. This handsome, talented man was that great rarity in New York fashion circles
and, indeed, fashion circles worldwide—a straight man, actually married, with children, living as
normal a family life as he and his wife could contrive, considering his work and position. Great
copy—up to a point.

Although always ready to talk about his clothes, his fashion philosophy, or his design concepts,
Ralph Lauren did not allow his private life to become public property. Some see such an attitude
as reflecting hubris, others integrity. But Lauren's friends believe that the price of privacy was
high. Ralph's clothes were good. Everyone acknowledged the fact. Often, they were superb. But his
name did not produce the "sexy" frisson that the names of higher profile designers did. The press
loves notoriety, not privacy. The fashion magazines always mentioned Ralph and his clothes, but
many observers felt that their coverage was a testimony to his healthy advertising budgets more
than an indication of where their hearts lay. And, in a strange way, Ralph Lauren almost feels a
degree of pleasure as well as resentment in what he sees as neglect. As he said in an interview for
The Washington Post, "Everything in this company was built out of integrity, not phoniness. Not
wining and dining fashion editors. I was not the kissy boy."

The seventies was the period when fashion designers became public property. Their personalities
were probed, their lives were put under the microscope, and every aspect of their existence
magnified out of all proportion. As a young couple, Ralph and Ricky's delight was to have a cheap
Italian meal followed by a movie or, even better, to stay home, have a cook in with a couple of
friends or members of the family, and listen to the latest Frank Sinatra LP. But now Mr. and Mrs.

Above left: Woody Allen and Diane
Keaton in *Annie Hall*.
Above right: Robert Redford in
The Great Gatsby.

Lauren were expected to play the social game. Eleanor Lambert, doyenne of fashion PRs, points out, "Ralph Lauren was an ideal person to be in the fashion world. He was a handsome young man. Not tall, but personable in every way—and totally compelling as a human being. But he's not a joiner by nature. He never seemed to have many friends in the fashion world. Even when he was just starting out, he was rather... how can I say? Not mysterious exactly, but very cautious, very... concentrated. I never felt he enjoyed small talk. He's not a mixer. He just hovers around the fashion world."

One of Ralph Lauren's long-standing personal friends is the architect Charles Gwathmay, whom he met 25 years ago. "We used to pass each other out running in the Hamptons," Gwathmay recalls, "and we kept saying 'hello.' Then we met at a charity event in New York and there was a very warm sort of chemistry between us. I sensed he didn't have—and didn't want— many intimate friends in the fashion world. He's sort of guarded, initially. He doesn't want his time or space invaded." John Fairchild, at the center of the fashion world as publisher of *Women's Wear Daily* and until his retirement in 1998, goes further, claiming that Lauren is "probably the most personally insecure designer in the business."

Fairchild's sharpness is significant. What he required from designers was copy for his publications. He saw the very ordinariness of the Laurens and their lifestyle as a sort of failure to live up to their new social position. He knew that, with only a little effort, Ralph Lauren could be a social designer, either like Bill Blass and Oscar de la Renta, pillars of New York fashionable society or, even more newsworthy, flirting in and out of Manhattan's louche underbelly in the way men like Calvin Klein and Halston did. The Laurens would have none of it. The press took them at their word and left them alone. It could have had serious consequences for Ralph Lauren had what he had created not been too big to be affected by New York's parochial attitudes. To use one of his favorite expressions, if the press didn't "get it" then the public were right there with him.

The fashion media did not ultimately make Lauren's name a household word. Entirely appropriately for a man who had fallen in love with the movies even before he was twelve years old and had remained in love for the rest of his life, it was the cinema that did this for him. Two years after introducing his womenswear, in a period when he was gearing up for maximum creative and retailing thrust, Ralph was asked to work on the men's clothing for a filmed version of F. Scott Fitzgerald's novel *The Great Gatsby*. It was almost a dream come true. As Marvin Traub points out, "Ralph had been looking for a way to flesh out his image on a larger screen." Now, literally, the screen was presented to him. The star was Robert Redford—who happened to be a friend of both Ralph and Buffy—"a Ralph Lauren guy if ever there was one," as Traub observed. He played Jay Gatsby, while Bruce Dean was Tom Buchanan and Sam Waterson, Nick Carraway.

Works of literature that perfectly capture the mood of a culture at a particular moment are few. In the nineteenth century, Zola and Balzac did it for France, Tolstoy for Russia, Dickens and Trollope for England and, merging into the twentieth century, Wharton and James for America. In the thirties Moravia captured the feel of Italy, as Waugh did in England. That is why they are still read today. But for Americans—and much of the rest of the world—the two books that have talismanic status are J.D. Salinger's *The Catcher in the Rye* and F. Scott Fitzgerald's *The Great Gatsby*. Like every other young man in the fifties, Ralph read the former and identified totally with Holden

The range of menswear collections
from spring and fall from the eighties.

The film *The Great Gatsby* offered the opportunity for Ralph to vindicate his vision of male excellence on a vast scale.

Caulfield and his contempt for "phonies." But *The Great Gatsby* was the seminal experience for him. Here was a book that paraded as self-evident what he himself believed, that American "class" was, despite its roots in English history, an indigenous growth, open to all. The novel's fictitious West Egg and the even swankier East Egg could be conquered, with effort and talent, by those who really wanted to. Even as a young man on the lowly level of selling ties to stores, Ralph Lauren had known that he absolutely wanted to live the life of the characters in *The Great Gatsby*, albeit as quietly and exclusively as Jay Gatsby himself. To call the novel his primer would be an exaggeration but that it was one of his greatest influences is undeniable. Naturally the opportunity to work on the film—to have his menswear showcased in the film of "his" book—seemed a gift from the gods for a 34-year-old increasingly hailed as the new golden boy of the fashion industry.

If his involvement with the movie was romantic, his appreciation of what the exposure would do for his career was entirely practical. As he said in an interview in 1974, the year in which the Paramount film was released, "It was very important professionally for me to do the clothes for *Gatsby*… the publicity has been terrific. Now a lot of people want Ralph Lauren clothes." It was not only exposure and sales that made it important for Ralph. It was almost a rite of passage, a coming home for him, taking him back to the twenties of his heroes Fred Astaire and the Duke of Windsor. It was more, too: the film of *The Great Gatsby* offered Ralph the opportunity to vindicate his vision of male excellence on a vast scale. Jeff Banks feels he understood exactly how important it was to Ralph. "He wanted to do *Gatsby* more than he wanted life itself," he claims, hyperbolically. "I've never seen him want anything more." It is very easy to see why. Like the book, the film is male-driven. What the men wear is infinitely more important than what the women are wearing—which is why many in Hollywood found it odd that the costume designer Theoni Aldredge, in order to save time, chose to farm out the men's wardrobe rather than the women's. The film was made under pressure. Aldredge was commissioned to design the costumes in March 1973 and, as Banks recalls, "They had to shoot that summer because they needed good weather for the party sequences which were filmed in Newport to resemble the great houses on Long Island— the Gold Coast, as it used to be called. Also Mia Farrow, who was playing Daisy, was pregnant and they only had a few months where they could disguise it."

Sal Cesarani had worked with Aldredge on a Broadway show for which Ralph Lauren clothing had been used. He invited her to meet Ralph and see his current collection. She went to the showroom and lost no time in asking Ralph to provide the men's clothes for the movie. As she said in an interview at the time of the film's release, "I fell in love with everything I saw. Ralph was already so into the period, we've only had to make minor adjustments." It was a vast undertaking. The Lauren organization had to provide clothes not only for the stars but also for the extras. It was a marvellous opportunity, but it was also a daunting challenge. As if filming a book described by T.S. Eliot as "The first step American fiction has taken since Henry James" was not enough, it had already been done twice before as a film: in 1927, when Jay Gatsby was played by Warner Baxter, and then again in 1948, with the part played by Alan Ladd. There was a further complication. Theoni Aldredge was the film's costume designer. Ralph Lauren was the provider of the wardrobes for the male actors. This meant the decisions were hers, their execution his. Part of his contract was that Ralph would receive no credit as designer, his role being described in the words "men's wardrobe by Ralph Lauren."

Buffy explains that Ralph's "old money" approach to male dress, much though it had in common with the spirit of the film, had arrived well before *The Great Gatsby* was made: "Way back, when I was working on *The Daily News Record*, I did a story on one of Ralph's very first suit collections where he did a belted back linen suit and the headline was 'The Look Comes Straight Off Gatsby's Lawn.'" Recalling the film she goes on, "*Gatsby* turned out to be a very unfortunate situation—for a lot of people. There was a very short time frame and it was a monumental undertaking but, of course, at the time we had *Gatsby* in the line. I mean, the look was there already. We not only had the mood, we had the fabrics, the beautiful shirtings and, above all, the silhouettes. You could walk into the showroom and say, with every justification, 'This is *Gatsby*!' Aldredge didn't design any of the men's costumes although she had approval and was thrilled that it was all there for her. She just said to me things like, 'Listen, I need sixty suits for all the extras. I need fifty tuxedos' ... for whatever it was, and I went through our clothing line, selected every fabric and then just randomly went through the size range from thirty-six short to forty-six extra long and made up suits so that the extras could come in and try them. They were all fabrics that were in our line; they were all styles that were in our line. Ralph defined the characters. I remember sitting down with Ralph and him saying to me, 'Okay, Nick should only wear single-breasted jackets and he should wear the belted backs. Redford's going to wear double-breasted vests and he should wear this round collar. Nick should just have the long collars without stays in them and wear a pin.' Ralph defined that: she didn't. There were only two things that were literally designed for the movie that weren't in our line: the pink suit, because we didn't have a pink flannel suit in our line, as you could well imagine, and the bathing costume in which *Gatsby* is shot, because it was an old-fashioned striped-wool, belted costume." Jeff Banks also remembers the bathing costume. "We had to make at least eight versions of it because there were little phials inside containing mock blood, with strings attached to them so that when he was shot the blood would come out. We had to have a new costume for each take because the costumes wouldn't dryclean." Banks best sums up what costuming the film meant in real terms. "The clothes weren't totally authentic but, then, how could they be? They were in production, to be worn by men at that time but *Gatsby* was a great moment for Ralph because it gave him the kind of recognition outside the industry that he had been seeking."

It also provided an unprecedented retailing opportunity, as pointed out by Jerry Magnin, who owned Lauren's Rodeo Drive Polo shop in Los Angeles, "Never in his wildest dreams could Ralph Lauren think they'd bring back *The Great Gatsby*." Magnin laid plans even before the film was released, organizing an instore promotion backed by a mail campaign inviting customers to "come see the clothes inspired by *The Great Gatsby*, done by Ralph Lauren, who did the men's clothes for the movie." Other than the publicity and the raised profile, *Gatsby* proved to be an end in itself. Fanciful journalists of the time, beguiled by Ralph's confessions of his deep and early love of movies, imagined designing for Hollywood becoming a significant aspect of the Lauren empire. Even if he had thought it a good idea—and, to this day, he denies that a career as a movie designer ever entered his head—Ralph Lauren was far too busy doing things the way he wished: that is, having total creative control in a way even the greatest costume designer never achieves. Cynics dismiss any romantic references to Ralph's love of the cinema and suggest that he was keen to do *Gatsby* only for the publicity it afforded his men's line — a claim strenuously denied by friends and colleagues. Great achievers are always opportunists and if there were an element of truth in the suggestion then Ralph Lauren must be deemed doubly blessed by the movie world: in 1977, his women's line was given even greater publicity when Diane Keaton chose to wear it in the film *Annie Hall*. Again, there was no specific designing involved. As Buffy says, "She put it together in her own way, combining this year's Ralph Lauren with vintage Ralph Lauren with vintage Diane Keaton.… She doesn't make a big fuss … she hates packaged looks or carbon copies. It's just her personal style, natural and easy.… What she personified is the very natural, very American easy look." It was a look that, after the film went on release, women worldwide also wanted.

Well before *Annie Hall*, Ralph Lauren's name was known across America. Interviews and commentary had inevitably followed his unique—and, to some, idiosyncratic—approach to dress for both men and women. He had become a master of the soundbite that had just the right edge of provocation but avoided outright arrogance. Fashion has always had a bad name; even those who love it cannot resist villifying it and, as Ralph made no effort to disguise his impatience with the fashion world while highlighting his belief in the normality of women and their dress needs, he had a groundswell of support, fed and encouraged by newspapers across the land. He was remarkably open, always prepared to give time to journalists even from newspapers that the smart New York fashion set pretended never to have heard of.

But it was more than that. The clothes themselves were so alluring. It is hard not to sound fanciful but they chimed so perfectly with the aspirations of so many Americans that to may they really seemed talismanic objects which, once possessed, would somehow improve and enhance the owner's life. Furthermore, Lauren's clothes made many buyers feel distinctly more American when

Below left and right: Ralph would often star in his own advertising campaigns.

A new tradition in *American western wear.*

It was made to be worn.

The Ralph Lauren Western Collection for men and women.

they wore them. How did he achieve such an effect? Most commentators believe it was the result of brilliant marketing, say 60 percent intuition, 30 percent calculation, and 10 percent chutzpah. And it worked. Rather too well. Far too many of the people who wanted the Polo label could not afford it and by the mid-seventies Ralph Lauren discovered the dark side of success. It seemed that every place he went he came face to face with 'knock-offs' of his Polo line—not necessarily badly done but not up to the standard of the original and, of course, appreciably cheaper than the authentic garments. He realized that he had to acknowledge the demand for the look and its cachet at a price that a much wider section of the buying public could afford. Retailers were crying out for the Lauren magic that they could sell at a more accessible price point.

To accommodate their needs, he created Chaps, a lower-priced trouser line which was launched in the mid-seventies to counter the 'knock offs' of Polo. It was a department store brand, not carried at Polo retail, and even though it has expanded beyond trousers, remains a department store brand. By its name and the advertising campaigns backing it, Chaps tapped into the most magical and mythical area of America, both historically and geographically. Ralph Lauren answered the call, not of the wild, but of the West, which was not only his own personal Nirvana but also spiritual home for millions of Americans from all classes in 1978 when he created his jeans-dominated range for men and women—Westernwear. At that time, the denim field was dominated by Wrangler and Levi Strauss but, fired by his love of the west and the cowboy aesthetic. As he explained in an interview in 1976, "The American heroes are John Wayne, Steve McQueen, and Levi Strauss. I want my clothes to combine ruggedness, purity and non-fashion… a way of being free, a philosophy of living… And the secret is to keep the character but do it with class."

Class and character: it was the perfect summation of what Ralph Lauren stood for in the eyes of middle America: The push to make Westernwear of root-and-branch importance in the Lauren design cannon was a move of brilliant prescience, hooking in to the whole cinematic iconography which ranged from *High Noon* and *The Gunslinger* to *Oklahoma* and *Carousel* and, incidentally, recalling Gertrude Stein's comment on America, made way back in 1934, as the place where "There is more space where nobody is than where anybody is. This is what makes America what it is."

Lauren was about to open a rich vein, his own Klondike. As he said in *GQ* in August 1978, "Western clothes are the most distinctively American of all clothing." His advertising campaigns were pushing the message home, most powerfully, perhaps, in those funded by his old champion, ale's. Trumpeting its "Ralph Lauren Week," to launch his westernwear collection, the copy was sassy and upbeat, its mood more state-fair jolly than Newport languid. Under the banner, "Ralph Lauren's Turning New York into a One-Horse Town … Now That's Cause for a Wing-Ding!" the copy missed no opportunity to link into the West and cowboy culture. "And wing-dinging we are," it continued, "Lauding everything Lauren with one riproarious celebration that salutes the man who blazed his first fashion trail with us back in '67. There'll be plenty to be seen and herd [sic] all week, beginning with Ralph himself at high noon tomorrow… with the debut of his West-is-best collections for men and women. Come in for a look-see at how the West was worn. And don't miss our windows—all 23 of them!" It says much for the profit that Bloomingdale's were making out of Ralph Lauren that they gave him such an unprecedented number of windows. Even if they

Ralph Lauren's Westernwear collection.

52

Class and character: it was the perfect summation of what Ralph Lauren
stood for in the eyes of middle America.

never read a word of the advertising copy, the many thousands of shoppers walking down Lexington Avenue couldn't fail to get the message that Ralph had brought the West to town—and sales proved that many agreed with his assertion that "Western clothes are very exciting and romantic." Not even his toughest critics were inclined to argue when he added, "I made Western wear very important. I pioneered it—and it's tremendously gratifying."

It was not easy to find critics. The fashion world sat back, open-mouthed at Ralph Lauren's irresistible rise. It began to look as if he could sell to Americans anything he wished. As Geraldine Stutz says, "You've got to realize that what was going on between Ralph and the American public—us, the American purchasers—was a very subtle thing. What he gave them—through his clothes but pre-eminently in his advertising campaigns—was the big outlines of a life. They weren't fooled any more than he was. They knew that it was a make-believe world. Do you think real life is like that? He gave them the perfection of make-believe. And Americans wanted it. That's what you have to understand."

Escapism can take any form, but it must be led by someone with a vision of a better world. Steve Bell believes that Ralph Lauren played Pied Piper to a nation because "he had total vision in terms of what he believes is the way of doing things. He's always had ferocious focus. He's the epitome of content and delivery—all that emotional intensity, single-mindedness, and egocentricity! And it starts in a very personal way. I've known lots of the people who've worked for Ralph over the years and I know that every single one of them feels that, when they're with him, they're the total focus of his attention, like, what they're saying to him is the most important thing in the world for him at that point. It's all focus." Charles Gwathmay adds, "Ralph's very insightful. It's not just that he is amazingly intuitive. He gets people's pulse."

Getting the pulse of a nation is, perhaps, no harder than doing so with friends and acquaintances. If the seventies were the decade of Ralph Lauren's first great thrust, they were a bad time for most Americans. The postwar economic boom and the youthful hope and enthusiasm of the sixties soured. Americans grasped at the thing they felt would give them hope: a return to the values that had made America not just a great nation but the greatest nation on the planet. "We are Americans" they seemed to say—something which, with uncanny prescience, Ralph Lauren (who has no interest in politics) had been saying throughout the decade. In interview after interview he reaffirmed his standpoint: "I am an American designer." His comments, advertisements, and, above all, product, celebrated his nation with the simplest and most direct of all emotional appeals: to the honesty, integrity and guts of America's own hero, its own simple universal man, unique to the nation's soil—the cowboy. But the celebration went wider. In a decade when New York, the supercity for the world, became a paradigm for urban decay, the wide-open spaces, clean air, and true values of rural America eluded to a life lived according to different, purer values. Lauren kept giving the American people glimpses of a better world. It was a romantic vision, but his fellow countrymen needed such a vision. They responded to the essential goodness of the Ralph Lauren world, based, as it seemed to be, on traditional values of rural America. Of course they bought the roughwear, Westernwear, hand-knit sweaters, leather and suede, noble tweeds, and fine linens, and paid a high price for them. They did so because, somehow, the clothes not only made them feel better but also gave them confidence. Ralph Lauren was in the right place at the right time with the right product. He did not plot and scheme. What made him so successful was that he knew purely by instinct what it was that people wanted from

Right: Ralph and Ricky attend the Coty awards, 1977.

Above: The original advertising imagery for the fragrance Polo.

clothes, simply because that was what he, his wife, and his growing family required (his eldest son, Andrew, had been born in 1969, his second, David, two years later and his daughter, Dylan, three years after that. Certainly he had a vision, and he was determined—even driven. But what gave Ralph Lauren his great success in the seventies was his normality. No fancy rhetoric. No flights of fantasy. Just a persuasive rubric that said, "You can make it better." Millions of Americans happily paid good money to buy into his conviction. As the decade drew to a close Polo Ralph Lauren had become much more than just a label on items of clothing. It represented an attitude of mind and a scale of values.

Ralph Lauren had been celebrated so warmly as the evangelist of dress that he had acquired a mystique totally separate and different from that of any other American designer. The mystique went beyond clothing. In October 1976 Warner Communications announced that they had joined with Lauren to work on developing fragrances—then, as now, virtually a license to print money, if packaging, price and fragrance are right. As Warner knew, no designer in America could better Lauren's profile. And as Ralph Lauren knew, nothing keeps a designer's name current more successfully than a range of fragrances.

As Marvin Traub says, fragrance was… "the conduit through which Ralph was finally able to communicate his vision to a mass public." That is why he had been pondering the idea of a scent for some time. Even so, he had repulsed several advances because he felt the deal was not right. What made the Warner's deal interesting when it was presented to him by George Friedman, an executive at Estée Lauder, was that, unlike the others, it was more than just selling his name as one of many in a company.

His scents would be a brand in themselves—the only thing a man with Ralph Lauren's temperament would consider. George Friedman knew this well enough. He recalls that he had first met Ralph "probably in the very early seventies. I was running Aramis for Estée Lauder, which was the first really great, upper-echelon, successful men's fragrance, and we were in the General Motor's building on Fifty-seventh and Fifth Avenue. I was on my way back from lunch when I ran into Neil Fox who was vice president of Neiman Marcus, and he was with Ralph Lauren. Now Ralph at that time was just getting to be famous for his ties and maybe some shirts, and Neil introduced me to Ralph, saying 'You know, you'll really like Ralph and he does some wonderful stuff' and Ralph said, 'Come and see my things.' I went over, I probably bought some ties, we had lunch, and we became friends. We had similar backgrounds, he grew up poor in the Bronx and I grew up poor in Brooklyn, we both had visions, and we began regularly to have lunch and walk through Central Park with a hotdog. He knew, and I knew, he had something of enormous value, and that was the name Polo. At that point in time we were looking at Lauder, who owned Aramis, to do a second men's fragrance, and Polo was a natural. It was the quintessential establishment name and so, as Ralph and I got to know and like each other, I went to the Lauder family and I said, 'This should be the next brand.' But I never could get them to agree. In those days the Lauders were a little chary of mixing their name with someone else's. So, for the next three or four years, Ralph and I maintained our friendship and every time another company would approach him, and offer a deal to do a fragrance, I would find a way to kill it. And I would keep on resuscitating the idea with the Lauder family and it never worked. I got increasingly frustrated and Ralph said to me, 'You're never going to leave,' and I said, 'No, no I will. I want to start my own company with you.'"

When the Warner offer arose, Ralph talked to Friedman, who went back to Lauder to see if they might be interested. They were not, so he left. The Lauder family insisted, as part of the release deal, that Friedman would not launch a competitive fragrance for at least a year. The new company was called Warner/Lauren and Friedman was chairman and CEO. The year's embargo proved a blessing in disguise. He explains, "As we had a year, we decided to develop a man's and a woman's fragrance at the same time, something which had not been done before. Also, we used the embargo time to our advantage: we traveled around the United States, visiting every department-store president and preselling."

Both fragrances were launched simultaneously, on March 23, 1977: Polo was the men's fragrance and Lauren the women's. Polo became much stronger than Lauren. In Friedman's opinion it reflected the fact that, even in the late seventies, Ralph Lauren's name was still more directly linked with menswear than with women's. Until 1984, when the company was sold to L'Oreal, the two men worked together. It was an essentially relaxed partnership: "We didn't live too far from each other and we used to run together in the park—which is when we had our meetings. I'm two or three years older than Ralph and I remember once I ran five miles and Ralph was all for running another five so I said, 'Ralph, we've got to find another way. I can't have these long meetings with you any more!'"

The venture was successful and the company went on to introduce Chaps, a cheaper but equally successful fragrance for men. A cosmetics line followed but failed to take off. It was a minor setback for Ralph Lauren and his dream. As he entered the eighties, he was confident that he had learned what he needed to about designing, marketing, and publicizing his product. He was ready to expand into the new areas that he had never quite had enough time to think about up until then.

getting the look

The eighties were the time when British class—a comfortably amorphic concept—made serious inroads into the American visual sensibility, making Ralph Lauren one of its major beneficiaries. As upper-class lifestyles were paraded on cinema and television screens, it became apparent to thousands who had previously misunderstood aspects of Lauren's zeitgeist—or, indeed, failed to comprehend at all—just what it was that he was offering. His message was not merely about clothes. It was equally about attitudes. It presupposed a desire in the public for grace, elegance, understatement, taste—all the things traditionally associated with the assurance of the upper classes, American, as much as British.

Lauren has been accused of many things: plagiarizing the past, glorifying colonialism, encouraging snobbery, failing to face the realities of the world, and, above all, plundering past cultures with little or no sensitivity. Each accusation requires to be answered, but the point that is usually lost is the extraordinary prescience of the man. As early as the seventies he was suggesting attitudes that did not fully enter the general consciousness until the eighties. He was literally years ahead of his time. In both his men's and women's ranges, he made his mark by basing his collections on upper-class ways of life, as he had seen it through the medium of film. His achievement is that of a culturally intuitive, almost accidental, man who has somehow absorbed a complex artistic background without having any identifiable or obvious links with it. It is undeniable that Ralph Lauren, uniquely in American fashion, is part—and a mainstream part—of his country's literary and artistic movement.

"The old qualities of living inspire me, but much as I love an old fifties Jaguar car, I am thrilled by today's high-tech Porsche."

The creative tradition continued by Ralph Lauren is that of the Euro-Americans, a group with a cultural importance beyond the shores of America. Usually wealthy, they had the urbanity that travel imparts and they were generally as familiar with the West End of London and the more chic arrondissements of Paris as they were with the mansions of Newport, Rhode Island. Their great moment was in the last years of the 19th century and the first years of the 20th, when the spiritual soil of hundreds of years was being turned, ready for the seeds of the people's century. They were the days when men like John Pierpoint Morgan, John D. Rockefeller, William B. Astor, and the whole group of entrepreneurs condemned by Theodore Roosevelt, not entirely justly, as malefactors of great wealth, were living gilded lives of ostentation and rivalry, vying with each other to have the grander home, the larger yacht, and the more bejeweled wife, not to mention the greatest art collection. Joseph Duveen paid Bernard Berenson handsomely to plunder the art of Europe on his behalf; in 20 years Pierpoint Morgan spent the modern equivalent of $900 million on building his peerless art collection. It was a period when appearances were paramount.

It was also a period when the fountainheads of taste and style were considered to flow with the greatest purity in Britain. Victoria's long reign had convinced the world that her country was superior in most things but certainly in grace, behavior, and style. The center of female elegance was undoubtedly Paris, but masculine mores sprang from the arcane rules of the British court, clothes of a perfection that the entire world felt could only be found in Savile Row. Whether a man lived in Philadelphia or Milwaukee, if he had any aspirations to being a gentleman of style, he followed the London way. As the shrinking coffers of the English aristocracy were increasingly bolstered by substantial injections of American money through wise and mutually beneficial dealings—for her, a title; for him, a bank balance to be reckoned in millions—so American family and friends of the newly married heiress discovered the true facts of English upper-class life. They learned of the cultural hinterland, known as "the country," where men dressed in no way less ritualistically than they did in town but in clothes that appealed much more to their egalitarian new relations, as appearing—erroneously—almost classless in their universality.

Tweeds, waterproofs, and brogues of a quality that ensured that they did not just last a lifetime but could be worn by generations of the same family, introduced a new concept not only of quality and style, but of antiquity. It was country dress which gave the Englishman his horror of clothing that was new. Whereas the pristine and the perfect were accepted as correct in Bond Street and St. James's, anything new in the country smacked of the *arriviste*. If the idea of fashion in male dress was frowned upon, the idea of fashion change in country clothes was almost inconceivable. There is an old joke concerning two dukes meeting in London's Pall Mall. One says to the other, "That suit is disgracefully old." He is told, "Oh, it doesn't matter, nobody knows me here." Two weeks later, the same pair meet on a shoot, the second duke wearing the same suit. Remonstrated with again, he replies, "Oh, it doesn't matter. Everybody knows me here."

The anecdote sums up an arrogant disregard for opinion that was dear to the heart of the aristocratic British male in the early years of the twentieth century. He was nervous of newness and only relaxed when items of dress were "broken in." There are endless tales, not necessarily all apocryphal, of suits of plus fours constructed—or "built" as Savile Row tailors termed it, appropriately enough for such monumental and heavy pieces of work—to last a lifetime being

promptly given to a trusted ghillie to wear until the newness wore off; of brogues splashing through Highland bogs on the feet of a servant until sufficiently worn to be seen on the feet of the duke.

Ralph Lauren instincitvely understands such thinking. As he says, "In America, if a sweater has a hole in it, you throw it away; in England, you keep wearing it until you pass it on to your son." From the very beginning, when he first began with his men's range, he worked on the principle that quality does not just last, but actually improves with time. To obtain this quality he turned to the woollen mills of England in the West Country, Yorkshire, and the North; he bought his cotton from Lancashire mills, his tie silk from Macclesfield, and his tweeds from Scotland. He also had most of the materials made up in the United Kingdom.

Lauren has been accused of being too English in his creativity, but the accusation does not stand up to investigation. His fashion thinking is, like the writing of James or the painting of Sargent, unmistakably the product of an American sensibility, albeit observing and reflecting a British attitude. Again like James and Sargent, his great skill lies in maintaining the integrity of the European quality of his clothes without sacrificing their American feel—just as tailors in every

Above: The confidence and poise of the
perfectly groomed.

American city with a sophisticated clientele have tried to do, just as Brooks Brothers and every Ivy League dress supplier have done. Lauren's skill has been to take these strands to create a look that may well start in the past but is essentially modern. "I have always been an experimenter," he claims. "I am inspired by heritage, English values, books, and sports, and I bring them all together in my designs. Overall, yes, the old qualities of living inspire me but, much as I love an old fifties' Jaguar car, I am thrilled by today's high-tech Porsche."

Upstairs, Downstairs had appeared on their television screens in the sixties, along with *The Forsyte Saga*, both landmarks in the promulgation of English class attitudes and moral approaches. Then had come *Brideshead Revisited*, a requiem for a world already vanished. Merchant Ivory began its long homage to English literature and the ways of the upper class, as seen in films like *A Room with a View*, released in 1986, although David Putnam's 1981 movie *Chariots of Fire* more precisely echoed the attitudes of Ralph Lauren just as 1994's *Legends of the Fall*, starring Brad Pitt and Julia Ormond in the peerless setting of Montana, brought the wheel full circle with a perfect evocation of exactly where Ralph Lauren had first begun, in the very early seventies.

For Ralph Lauren, even as a young man, the way the Duke and Duchess of Windsor dressed exemplified what he believed in. He loved the dedication to perfection that compelled the Duke to have his jackets tailored in England but his pants made by an American tailor. He saw him as a modern Beau Brummel, a man for whom no trouble was too great, provided the end result was right. For Ralph, it was not just the perfection of cut that characterized all the Duke's clothes, even at their most casual; it was the supremely relaxed way in which he wore them. No matter what the occasion, he never looked like a tailor's dummy. The clothes never dominated the man. It is the essence of the Ralph Lauren philosophy of dress.

He has never hidden his dislike of fashion which, in its positions and exclusions, he considers artificial and unreal. He loves the way things gradually develop—a way of tying a belt here, the angle of a hat there. It is the strength of the random as opposed to the contrived which he so loves, finding it in that glowing area where fashion is transformed into style.

The glamor of the Duke of Windsor and the streamlined simplicity of photographs of the south of France find their full fruition in the movies, specifically the comedy of manners which was a staple of Hollywood in the thirties and forties, a time when good films were made in black and white, which gave them a visual power not often captured today. The roll call of movies that helped to form Ralph Lauren's visual sense includes classics of the caliber of Clark Gable and Claudette Colbert's *It Happened One Night*, directed in 1934 by Frank Capra, who, two years later, shot Gary Cooper in *Mr. Deeds Goes to Town*, and James Stewart and Katharine Hepburn in *The Philadelphia Story*, released in 1940. Add movies like *Mrs. Miniver* and *Woman of the Year*, and the sophisticated nature of the training received by the Lauren eye becomes apparent.

It was not solely Lauren's approach to dress that was being educated. He was also learning about the importance of sophisticated surroundings—"woodies" with whitewall tyres rolling up to country clubs; luxurious, mirrored bathrooms with toweling robes as thick as a fur coat; drawing rooms furnished with long, comfortable sofas and elegant table lights at just the right height; and, inevitably, in a burgeoning consumer society, kitchens with the most streamlined and sophisticated of electrical appliances. They made the ideal setting for the perfectly cut clothes of

"I am inspired by heritage, English values, books, and sports, and I bring them all together in my designs."

Elements of style in Ralph Lauren country.

Above: Fall 1981.

the actors: the man-tailored suit worn by Loretta Young at the races in the 1938 movie *Kentucky*; the entire wardrobe worn by Gene Tierney in Otto Preminger's 1944 blockbuster *Laura*; and, quintessentially, the assured relaxation of the wardrobes of Katharine Hepburn and James Stewart in one of Ralph Lauren's favorite movie, *The Philadelphia Story*. They add up to an impeccable visual education, and Ralph Lauren draws on his memories of them in much the way that Yves Saint Laurent constantly recharges his imagination by returning to the world of Diaghilev. For both men, their early visual education has been the basis of all they have achieved.

The sources of creative inspiration tell much about the person who uses them and Lauren's movie references are both highly focused and limiting. For all his life he has responded more to the products of the lens than the easel. His imagination is not stirred by a painting of a courtesan by Fragonard but it can be deeply excited by a photograph by Edward Steichen. A boulle cabinet moves him very much less than a leather-and-steel armchair by Le Corbusier. He can admire but not relate to a grand palace like Caserta but can be deeply moved by a minimalist masterpiece such as Richard Meier's Douglas House. The result is that Lauren's reference points are almost exclusively 20th century. Even when he falls in love with the beauty of an eighteenth-century English home, sitting placid and pretty in a landscape equally as old, it is not with the eighteenth-century denizens that he identifies but with the people who lived there in the thirties and who live there today. What he finds appealing are modern lives lived in comfortably aged surroundings.

There is one exceedingly important exception to this broad rule. It is the culture of his own country, especially as found in Santa Fe, Taos, the Adirondacks, the Prairies, and the West, all of which reflect the outdoor life, barely changing except in response to the seasons; the life of action; the masculine life; the life that frequently revolves around the horse. Lauren often takes a 19th-century romantic view. The wild, open spaces where man is confronted with—and often humbled by—nature is where, in his vision, men come to terms with themselves and each other, and thus grow and mature. But Lauren's view is also contemporary. For him, a cowboy does not necessarily sacrifice any of his integrity simply because he is driving a pick-up truck rather than riding an Appaloosa stallion. This integrity appeals to him because he sees it as being based on values which have not been corrupted by modern life. Most importantly, Lauren responds to the integrity of items of dress that have developed as practical solutions to the problems of the outdoor life, clothes that have evolved almost organically in answer to certain situations: the cowboy's chaps or bandana, the fisherman's waders and broad hat, the tough boots and fur hat of the Arctic hunter. For Ralph Lauren they have the natural elegance that comes from fitness of purpose and to him they are more beautiful than any "designed" fashion look, sharing with machines the total harmony of form that has arisen from the needs of function. It is, for him, the same integrity that informs the log cabin built by the hands that felled and prepared the timber.

This integrity is not confined to men's clothing. When Ralph and Ricky took their children to Santa Fe in the early eighties they were excited by the possibilities afforded by native American crafts such as pottery, beadwork, weaving and silverwork. The stimulus resulted in one of Ralph Lauren's most successful collections. Santa Fe was a celebration, with sweaters based on native American Navaho blankets and textiles, fringed jackets and silver conch belts. It was followed by Americana, a celebration of the American-ness of traditional American dress. In it models wore demure "schoolmarm" blouses with flounced and laced collars, patterned, hand-knit sweaters, skirts made from antique American quilts—which caused accusations at the time that he was

Above left and right: Cruise 1992.

Overleaf: Fall 1990.

squandering a historical resource not easily renewed—beautiful fringed jackets, finer by far than any that ever graced a cowboy's back a hundred years previously and blanket coats inspired by Navaho Indian blankets. But the interest the West sparked in Lauren went beyond clothes to take in the indigenous skills of much more of America. In 1988, for example, Ralph Lauren sponsored the 10th anniversary of The Fall Antiques Show at the Pier in New York. One of the advertisements in the catalog carried a quote from Robert Henri's book *The Art Spirit*: "Order is perceived by the man with a creative spirit. It is achieved by the man who sincerely attempts to express himself and thus follows organic law." It so perfectly summed up Ralph Lauren's creative beliefs, it might have been written about—or even by—him.

It is this timelessness, this feeling that modernity only has meaning if it is part of a design continuity going back well beyond the period of the designer himself, that inspires Lauren's approach. It has been—and still is—his strength but it is also his cross. Ralph Lauren has been so successful because he has always had a total commitment to his vision. He is distressed when the suggestion is made that, as a designer, he is interested only in surface, with no substance to back it up. Even more, he is perplexed when people imply that he is not a designer at all, but merely a stylist. For many in the world of fashion these views have become almost holy writ, repeated without thought or reflection. They stem from two sources: the fact that, being unable to draw, Lauren does not make the sketch, the first step in the design process; and the fact that the clothes he designed in the seventies were so successful that lazy people see them as his archetype and use them to blind themselves to his many achievements since.

It seems hard that the very success of a man should become an albatross around his neck, but Ralph Lauren is not the only designer to suffer in this way. Ralph Lauren is hoisted on the petard of his success in so perfectly capturing the mood of his time. Much of his design production is classified as classic, but this falsifies his career by ignoring his other achievements. His clothes are classically minimalist, the result of a brain as much an engineer's and historian's as an artist's. But it is no more faithful to the truth than today's assessment of Chanel which, ignoring her brilliant—and diverse—designing career in the years between the wars, considers her only as the creator of the Chanel suit in the early fifties.

Ralph Lauren's early collections in both men's and womenswear had a heritage quality. They looked back, but they avoided being mere costume because they also looked forward. Ralph Lauren is not Laura Ashley, whose success was based on a concept so limited that it had no possibility of expansion. Nor is he a Mary Quant or André Courreges, whose statements were so of their moment that they died with that moment. Lauren's career has lasted for over three decades because he has moved with those decades. It is unsound to criticize him for consistency—especially when, within the boundaries of his viewpoint on fashion, the sexes, and how life should be led, he has been as full of design variety as any designer must be who creates clothes and other artefacts to actually be sold, rather than merely provide a brief talking point.

Lauren's approach to design is fundamentally practical, the result of his response to the simple questions all designers should ask. In Ralph's case, for his menswear collections, he asks, "How do my sons and I wish to dress?" For his women's collections, it is "How do my wife and daughter wish to dress?" For his home collections, the question is, "How do my family wish to live?" From

this domestic microcosm, he pulls away, taking the broader view, encompassing other needs. The practical base is always the beginning. Only after that do beauty, grace, elegance, and sophistication—all hallmarks of Lauren the designer—come into play. For Ralph Lauren all design is a response to problem-solving. Only from this approach can he answer the questions—"What is wanted?" "What will reflect this moment?"—that inform his collections each season. The design energy that enables him to produce so many collections each year comes from the fact that they are all carefully judged variations on an equally carefully considered theme. Ralph Lauren is far too mature and focused to make his statement in the way so many designers do, by responding to the trivial questions, such as "How can I be different?" "How can I be new?" Such considerations would never enter his head. He is a man with a vision, and it is a consistent one.

The other established criticism of Lauren—that he does not draw—is even more fundamental, being an overt attack on his design integrity. The argument is based on the assumption that dress designers must express their ideas on paper. Ralph Lauren does not do this. Instead, he works with sketchers who are so attuned to his fashion approach that they are able to interpret his wishes after only a couple of sentences. Who, in this case, has been the designer: the man who gives the instructions or the sketcher working on those instructions? If we broaden the picture with other examples it becomes apparent that the argument that insists that design can only be valid if it is "hands on" is specious. Is a composer less of a composer if he cannot play the instruments for which he writes? Did Brunelleschi need to know how to carve before he could design a dome?

Critics of Lauren as a designer are working on premises that do not survive logical examination. Although the sketch is the basis of design, it is not important who executes that

Below left: Fall 1983.

Below right: Themes and variations.

sketch, so long as it contains the spirit of the designer's thoughts. With some European designers putting their name to as many as 40 different collections per season, it would be grotesque to try to pretend that the individual whose name is on the label had sketched every idea—or even the main one. Designers, once successful, have many more demands on their time than sitting for several days sketching their ideas. Many don't draw, several rely on computer graphics. None of them—with the possible exception of Yves Saint Laurent—work in what would today be seen as a hopelessly inadequate, anachronistic way which, even in the romantic haze that surrounds designers of the past, cannot be substantiated. Chanel, that busy self-publicist so dedicated to contention, rarely wasted her time in sketching, although Christian Dior used it to clarify his ideas. Vionnet and Balenciaga preferred to design on the form, their tools a bolt of cloth and a pair of shears. Only when they had achieved in toile what they wished to create was the idea sketched, not in order to make a pretty picture but to form a record and help the workrooms to achieve what the designer required. Even a designer with a hand as fluent as John Galliano rarely sketches. Instead, designers have teams who, working on a brief which can be as vague as a picture from an old magazine, as specific as the work of another designer, or as amorphous as a few moments' discussion about mood, will then produce many hundreds of drawings while the designer is doing other things. Increasingly, modern designers are instigators and reactors, not illustrators.

This is exactly how Ralph Lauren should be described. To talk of him as somehow inferior to his counterparts in Europe is to demean a man whose impact on fashion, and on the way women actually dress—by no means the same thing—is enormous. His sales figures are proof of his success in judging what they require. In his company report for the fiscal year 2000, net revenues were approximately $1.96 billion, a growth from $1.03 billion a mere four years earlier. His clothes are chosen by more people than those designed by many French designers all put together—and the reason lies in their essential wearability. The person with whom Ralph Lauren most closely shares a fundamental design philosophy is Chanel. Like her, he believes that, although clothes must be logical, they can also be magical. Chanel's severely practical approach, down to the slim chains sewn in the hems of skirts to make them hang correctly, did nothing to destroy the beauty of her clothes. Ralph Lauren is entirely in the tradition she established. Like her, his instinct is never to add but always to subtract in order to make a statement clean, modern, and worldly.

Lauren will be remembered because he has altered our perceptions—of ourselves, our possibilities, and even our importance. Through his unrivaled eye and unwavering vision he has helped teach us about taste, harmony, and grace. Lauren has opened the eyes of millions who began to see things differently as a result of his lead. He continues to do so—as do his imitators, a group that ranges from The Gap to Martha Stewart and most importantly Tommy Hilfiger. This is not to suggest that they copy Ralph Lauren. Rather, they have taken on board and understood his concepts, using them to help them form their own. Whether or not Ralph Lauren sees this as a form of plagiarism or merely an example of opportunism, he surely cannot fail to accept the old aphorism that imitation is the sincerest form of flattery.

Such imitation is not always benign. It seems that everybody wants the Polo product, preferably without paying the Polo prices. Like many names—Chanel, Gucci, and Prada—that are household words even in societies where what they actually stand for—taste, power, and wealth—has little meaning, pirated versions of Ralph Lauren's product are sold cheaply and illegally worldwide, in markets, bazaars, and even on the streets of sophisticated Western cities. Like other

Overleaf: **Fall 93 and 94.**

Pages 74 and 75: **Pure elegance.**

designers fighting this trade, it costs the Lauren Organization a great deal of money every year. Lance Isham, corporate president and chief operating officer, sees it as part of the label frenzy that swept the world in the eighties and remains a potent force. But he also believes it reflects Ralph Lauren's achievement in taking the most stylish of clothes, from the twenties to the seventies, and making them better. Ralph Lauren, which manufactures many thousands of accessories, is especially vulnerable but Peter Strom, Lauren's partner and vice chairman until he retired in 1995, orchestrated a prudent damage limitation device by going into the countries where fraudulent merchandise was being manufactured and setting up bona fide Lauren manfacturing bases, thereby gaining the support of local governments in the battle to stamp out pirate factories. As Isham says, it was a first. No other company had explored this way of lessening, if not entirely killing, the damaging trade in fake products.

Nevertheless, Isham admits, "Although our trademark is registered in every country in the world, we still have serious problems with diverting merchandise whereby overproduction in manufacturing is sold to the secondary market without our approval and distributed illegally around the world. It is costly and time-consuming to keep track of this but it is possible to do so. We have ways of tracking where the garment was manufactured and how it is being distributed. So we do have some recourse when we find the products." The firm has a network of global checkers who go to flea markets and junk sales to search out fraudulent merchandise or third-party distribution so that the expensive business of eliminating the perpetrators can begin.

Above: Fall 1983.

The Polo Ralph Lauren look is global in every sense. Not only does it have a worldwide appeal but fabrics and raw materials are sourced across the globe, and manufacture takes place in many different countries. As Isham explains, "Our major sources are Italy for silk; woolens would be from Italy or Scotland; cottons could be American, Peruvian, or Indian. All of the really beautiful and expensive fabrics are, of course, European: Swiss, Scottish…. About ninety-five percent of all manufacturing for Purple and Black label is European. Men's shirts and womenswear are Italian."

This seems appropriate because, although Ralph Lauren is perceived as being essentially an American designer, his appeal is so clearly worldwide. There is barely an airline or airport shop that does not stock his perfumes. His chain of shops stretches from Chicago, where he has the biggest Polo Ralph Lauren store in the world, to Dubai, Sydney, and on to Mexico City.

In the last 20 years fashion has leapt over ethnic, religious, and cultural barriers in order to gain access to the enchanted garden of emergent nations and societies just beginning to become attuned to Western attitudes, all of which are eager for the fashion experience even when, as in certain countries in the Middle East, such enthusiasm is officially frowned upon. The promulgation of Western fashion becomes increasingly aggressive and all-pervasive, as designers attempt to create markets on a global scale. Stores promote designer garments with in-store boutiques, special events, fashion shows, and enticing window displays, in all of which the name and logo of the company is prominent. In such ways are markets created and encouraged. The image is vital. Clothes alone do not change fashion attitudes. Even the greatest designer must spend as much time conceiving how they are to be presented as how they are to be created.

Before Ralph Lauren, many designers failed to appreciate fully the importance of the marketing campaign as a significant—and indeed vital—selling tool. Their involvement was frequently peripheral, if they became involved at all. For most, to be actively involved was considered below

From the beginning, he was instinctively aware that label loyalty grows from identification not with a man alone but with a way of life.

the dignity of a creator. The briefing and overseeing of outside agencies who organized the advertising shoots was left to those working on the business and communications side of the fashion house. The designer's involvement was limited to briefing his staff and then approving the final result. It was not a hands-on experience. Ralph Lauren took the opposite stance. He has always been intimately involved with his advertising campaigns at all levels. He was one of the pioneers in understanding the vital importance of such campaigns as a link between product and consumer. But Ralph Lauren's contribution to the vernacular of fashion dialog has been the most significant. Twenty years after his breakthrough in this area, he pointed out to *The Wall Street Journal* in 1998, "I consider myself part of America's culture. I don't consider myself a designer … Business doesn't go up or down because I have a good or bad fashion show." What Lauren had realized was that if he could sell a lifestyle and an attitude of mind to people then sales of his clothes would follow automatically. In an extension of his approach to retailing, he set out to capture his customers' imagination rather than service their overt fashion needs.

Although he has subsequently been copied by so many others, Ralph Lauren was the first designer to take the approach that clothes must be portrayed in context and, further, that that context must convey a lifestyle. Even in the seventies, when he, Bloomingdales and Saks had decided that the focus of advertising campaigns should be the man as much as the merchandise, Lauren was taking a more imaginative and more intimate approach to his customers than any designer outside couture had ever done. The relationship between a couturier and his customer is a personal one, centred on the cabine of the couture establishment. As a ready-to-wear designer, Ralph could not hope for this same intimacy of two minds working together toward a single aim, but he understood instinctively that if he wished to engage the imaginations of women he would never personally meet, he had to find a way of guiding their thinking in the way a great couturier might do with an individual client.

Knowing that he was uncannily attuned to the aspirations of millions of men and women, he set about capturing their hearts and minds with advertising campaigns that were outstandingly bold in their imaginative insights. Clothes, by their nature, are ephemeral. Advertising campaigns last very much longer. They matched the aesthetic of the clothes which, as Buffy Birritella points out, have always been sufficiently "trendy" to be of the moment, yet classic enough to outlast the moment. As she says, Ralph Lauren's clothes are essentially "anti-fashion fashion." The way in which they are advertised reflects this. If Ralph Lauren clothes are the wardrobe for a lifestyle, the advertisements are less fashion photographs than glimpses into the world of that lifestyle. Birritella rightly claims, the photographs are doing much more than merely showing clothes.

Marvin Traub of Bloomingdale's understood as much as Ralph's colleagues had that the young tie salesman who had so successfully and quickly jumped the fence into full-scale retailing was, as the Elizabethans would say, a man of parts. Given a brilliant gift in his ability to visualize things down to the most minute of details, blessed with energy, drive, and a belief in the significance of his clothes and their power which could truly be called a vision, he had still more. What Traub saw was a man of great charm, the American equivalent of the continental boulevardier, a man who disarmed, who embraced people with the enthusiasm of his personality. In short, he saw that

Left: Fall 1990.

Above: One of the photographs taken by
Bruce Webber for *Harper's Bazaar*.

Ralph Lauren was his own best image for a company that was setting out to forge a loyalty base founded on personal involvement. Traub lost no time in capitalizing on the Lauren talents. Perhaps inspired by the success of the Saks campaign he encouraged Ralph to pose in his own advertising campaigns. He knew that the smile, the eyes, the aura of sexiness and masculinity would sell clothes to women just as successfully as a beautiful model could.

For Ralph, it was the beginning of a long involvement in his own campaigns. Like all designers, he has been photographed *ad infinitum*, frequently by some of the greatest photographers of the age. He has been caught informally by newspapers and paparazzi. He has posed in and out of studios. The results are almost always pleasing. The face that looks out at the viewer is friendly, candid, and reassuring. It normally smiles, and that can mean anything from the quizzical lift of one side of the mouth to a full-frontal grin. Only rarely does Ralph Lauren look straight at the camera with no attempt to ingratiate himself with the audience. He knows that his job in this role is to reassure and convince. He is aware that smiles sell, whether on a billboard, in a magazine, or in a half-page advertisement in the style section of a major newspaper.

But the Ralph Lauren eye is an idealizing eye. It is fine to let people see what sort of a man he appeared, but he knows that there are other, more subtle, ways of creating customer loyalty. From the beginning, he was instinctively aware that label loyalty grows from identification not with a man alone but with a way of life. He realized that what people wanted to have presented to them was a lifestyle. "He was first in the field with lifestyle advertising," Buffy Birrittella insists. "Nobody had ever thought of creating a world before Ralph did it. It was totally ground-breaking." For Ralph it was about authenticity, integrity and clothes that improve with age. He was inspired by heartland America, old tweeds rugged work clothes and old flannels. Rob Freda, who worked as a menswear designer for Polo Ralph Lauren in the nineties, points out how precisely Ralph has captured and presented these worlds of privilege in a way that opens them up to multitudes. "For somebody who didn't go to prep school," he claims, "Ralph has a perfect understanding of preppie. You know, that laid-back, floppy aspect of it. He has never had in his head the concept of the perfectly dressed collegiate type. You know, wearing your grandfather's clothes, a little frayed at the elbows or on the collar of your shirt. The idea that corduroys don't really become anything until a few dogs have been sick over them. Ralph gets that to a T. And, of course, although there is that upper-class aspirational thing to his clothes and his advertisements, it isn't really Ralph. He is marketing aspirations but he's not overly impressed by it all. Ralph is what you might call a true aristocrat. In spirit, he is European in that in the feudal system aristocratic status came through achievement. Getting it right on the battlefield could earn you a knighthood and Ralph has been getting it right creatively since the very beginning."

Ralph Lauren had the style, he had the vision, he had the product—but he needed somebody to realize it all for his advertising campaigns. In the photographer Bruce Weber he found a man with whom he would enjoy one of the most creative relationships in twentieth-century fashion promotion, a relationship that continues as intensely today as it did when they first began to work together in the late seventies. "It started in a crazy way," Weber recalls. "The art director of *Harper's Bazaar* phoned and asked me if I would like to photograph Ralph Lauren and his family for the magazine. I knew a bit about him and his clothes but nothing about him as a man. I got to know him by photographing him. It was really fun doing the pictures because the kids were still quite small then."

Above: Fall 1977.

Shared attitudes brought the two men together. "Ralph and I connected right at the beginning because we both loved clothes and we both loved cars, especially old sports cars. We used to joke that as a kid growing up in Pennsylvania I always wanted to have a Triumph, an MG, or especially an Austin Healey, but Ralph always felt my character needed a sharper car, like a Porsche." It was more than cars that made the men bond. Both wished to celebrate America through its own clothes, and that also produced a creative link between them. "In the early days," Weber says, "Ralph often used to come on a sitting with us and we would go shopping to thrift stores. He was so frustrating to go shopping with because he would feel thousands of things in the store until he'd found the best pair old of jeans and the best vintage leather jacket. Even if we went earlier, he would still stroll up later and find the bargain."

Weber has always enjoyed working with Lauren because he sees the process as more like making a film than doing a standard fashion shoot, although he admits that there is no such thing as a standard approach with Ralph. For him, Lauren approaches a campaign rather as the director would approach a film. "Everything in his movies was picturesque and every detail counted. Ralph has the same sense of complete detail. That's one of the reasons I respect him so much. Anyone who came in from the outside world would ask, 'Why are we doing this? Is a button so important?' And the answer is yes, for Ralph it is very important. When I'm photographing, I'm not just thinking of the clothes. I'm thinking of the man and his extraordinary creative generosity as well as that desire to be ahead. He always wants to be the first to take the path. Never the follower." Mary Randolph Carter, known throughout the Polo company simply as Carter, is senior vice president of advertising. She substantiates Weber's view. "Ralph absolutely does not like to follow."

There is an intuitive sense in Ralph Lauren, as there is in many designers. In his case, it takes the form of knowing what to do for any particular moment. Weber instances the time when they were discussing a photographic shoot and Ralph suddenly said of the men's suits, "'Why don't we photograph them on gorgeous girls? That will go someplace.'" And he was right, Weber maintains, because he was not simply thinking of selling things but of taking a different path. In the early days there were many meetings to discuss the concept for an advertising campaign but now both men are so attuned that they often do no more than exchange views over the telephone. "It frequently starts with Ralph saying, 'I've been thinking about this kind of character…' or 'I read in this book…' or 'I saw this movie….'" Then it becomes like casting a film. Weber makes suggestions, Lauren makes suggestions, Buffy makes suggestions, Carter adds her opinion. Sandy Carlson of Carlson and Partners Advertising, the firm that has worked exclusively with Polo for the past twenty years on its campaigns, also has an important voice. Discussion will focus on models, locations, and choice of garments for the shoot.

Pat Christman, currently vice president of corporate archives for Polo Ralph Lauren—a vast and well-documented record of all fashion shoots and campaigns the firm has done—was, like Buffy Birrittella, working on the campaigns in the eighties, when vast and costly shoots took the team to many parts of the world. An ex-model, she was responsible for what was the earliest archetypal Lauren image: the cowboy-hatted, tuxedo-wearing, dinner-suited man in an overcoat leading a horse across the snow. "It was in July 1977, and the photograph was taken by my ex-husband," she recalls. "We were living in LA at the time so we had to go to Montreal to find some snow. We had only one day to do it. The hat belonged to Ralph, who had lent it to me specially. I knew it was precious to him so I wore it throughout the flight. People thought I was nuts but I couldn't risk losing it! The crew consisted of me, my husband, and the model, who was called Clement, plus a pile of coats. Somehow, we found the last remaining sliver of snow in Montreal. It was a miracle. Ralph really loved that picture. He still does. In meetings it comes up regularly— 'Clement in the 'snow'—when he is explaining a mood he wants."

Not all archetypal images are created in a few hours on a crowded day. Fashion shoots are kept as loosely organized as possible in order that the people on site can have the maximum flexibility to obtain the unexpected, unscheduled shot—something for which Bruce Weber is famed. Both in the early days and today Ralph Lauren sets the tone and is fully involved in planning the shoot but now, having established his standards and requirements, he knows he doesn't always have to attend, safely leaving his team to carry out his detailed instructions. The exigencies of his life preclude a hands-on approach to advertising campaigns these days but he sets the mood and the final choice of images is his. As Pat Christman says, "Ralph tells us what he wants us to shoot and explains the feeling he is after. Because magazines close their advertising pages three months before publication we have to move quite quickly. We sit down with him pretty soon after the show so that he can explain what he wants."

While he has been preparing clothes for the show, Ralph Lauren has also been considering how he wants his collection to be presented in his advertisements. When he meets his staff, he already has certain things in mind, usually including the photographer and sometimes the models. As Pat explains, "He'll say, 'I've been thinking, and I really think this is Bruce,' or 'You know, I think Sheila Metzner would be really right for this.' For the women's line, Collection, he will pick ten looks and say, 'That's what I want my statement to be and Mario can shoot it.'" Carter goes a little further: "Ralph always puts himself in the position of the people who will be looking at his advertising. He never talks down to them. He gives his public a great deal of credit and he certainly doesn't imagine that they expect—or should have—the same 'Ralph Lauren' thing each time. For instance, his collection for Spring 2000 was shot by Mario Testino and that was quite a departure. He agonized a while over the choice but the collection was so hip and cool, with a lot of color, and he felt that Mario could bring something to that. But he also knew it was a risk and he might be giving up some of his heritage."

Lauren has always believed that a picture should so capture the Lauren image that it is almost unnecessary to put his name on it. One of his favorite questions when he and his team are deciding which pictures to use is, "Does this say Ralph Lauren? Is this a Ralph Lauren image?" But to merely ask that would soon lead to complacency and predictability, pitfalls of which he is constantly aware. The Testino pictures were very successful from a retail point of view because they attracted a younger, hipper customer into his stores, but he did not cry, "Eureka!" and assume that this was what Ralph Lauren was now all about. As Carter says, "Ralph is always aware that the real test is the test of time. He would never crawl into a trendy trap which might block his development. He wants his name and his clothes to endure." He has ensured that they do so by creating over the years a portfolio of iconic images that are a testimony to his boldness. Lauren was the first designer to realize that it is possible to evoke the spirit of clothes without actually showing any clothes, if the conviction is powerful enough. "He sticks to his guns," Carter says, "even when others are doubtful." A full-page picture of a bowl of roses ... a perfectly groomed

"Nobody had ever thought of creating a world before Ralph did it.
It was totally ground-breaking."

Spring 1984.

"A Bruce Weber shoot for Lauren resembles a film set more than anything else …"

Above: **Creating a mood.**

horse's head … three terriers on a back seat of a car … the side of a clapperboard barn shrouded in mist … a herd of stallions …. These are the images that Lauren uses as confidently as he does images of merchandise because he trusts his customers to be sufficiently attuned to his sensibility to understand the attitude and mood he is presenting. They are his passport photographs, proclaiming who he is, but he knows he cannot afford to be precious about preserving his image. "With the Testino picture people thought he had given up some of his identity," Carter comments. "But, of course, he hadn't. What he had done was broaden his identity. We address each campaign, decide the need, and then choose the photographer—and eighty-five percent of the time it has to be Bruce."

Bruce Weber is a man of considerable charisma as well as confidence in his skills and his judgment, a confidence which is entirely justified. When, in a hundred years' time, historians of fashion are looking for the photographic images that sum up Ralph Lauren's fashion approach, it can be taken as read that every one they choose will be by Bruce Weber. The rapport between him and Ralph is based on the fact that he totally buys into the dream and entirely believes in the vision. As someone who once worked within the company points out, "Ralph likes 'all-American' guys, and they don't come more American than Bruce. He also responds to people who aren't afraid of him and, paradoxically perhaps, men are usually more overawed than women. Many are overwhelmed by his massive achievements." Bruce Weber himself says that, although the two men have kindred feelings on many things, there are some matters on which they differ a lot. "But I respect him so much," he says, "that even if he makes points and I don't entirely understand where he's coming from, I'll go along with it and try to explore it because I want to learn something from him. It's always been teamwork, in any case. Not just me and Ralph, but Buffy, Sandy, and incredible Pat, who knew so much about clothes. She taught me a lot."

"Slowly I began to understand what inspired Ralph, what made him excited. We shared things like that. Often very simple things. But it's the way he is with people that really made me relate. His generosity of spirit. How he really looks at people when he's talking to them. So when I went out to take pictures I always thought of the man and I tried to capture in the photographs the quality of Ralph. I wanted to bring back Ralph in the pictures I took. They're part of his life, the way he is living at any moment. There's always been a kindness and sweetness toward people in him, and even when I'm shooting in a really rich situation I'm always trying to capture that humaneness, because that's what's important in Ralph Lauren."

From the beginning Weber would spend many days, even weeks, shooting campaigns for Ralph Lauren, the results often being presented in portfolios of up to twenty pictures in top magazines. The photographs were about moods and attitudes, and were both expansive and luxurious in the leisurely way in which they presented what Ralph Lauren stood for. In the nineties, product-focus became more direct, although the discursive, anecdotal approach was not forgotten. Today, Ralph Lauren continues to create advertising campaigns with a cinematic quality. The latest campaign— Fall 2002—recaptures the sensibility which has for so long been associated with Lauren. Like the Cliveden, Safari and American West campaigns, they are cast like a movie with models who will play their roles in ongoing situations in future campaigns, exactly like different scenes in a film. But iconic items are still given high focus. When Ralph Lauren first launched his range of paints, he used Irving Penn to photograph the paint can. Neither does this approach preclude the romantic style that has characterized his greatest campaigns. To capture something so amorphous demands

time, effort, and a sympathy in which Ralph Lauren believes deeply. The teams who go out to capture his dream for him—including models, hairdressers, and make-up artists—are all people who have worked on many of his campaigns, understand the ethos, and see themselves as belonging to the loose-knit but privileged "family" that Ralph Lauren has created.

Pat Christman calls them "the team" and admits that, certainly in the past, the numbers involved could be daunting. "A Bruce Weber shoot for Lauren resembles a film set more than anything else, including, as it can, as many as twenty people actively on site, with Bruce alone bringing up to four assistants. We have hair and make-up and, if we're using ten models of all different shapes and sizes, plus kids, their assistants as well. Then, if we have dogs, we need dog handlers. In total, on the whole site there might be thirty or forty people, what with drivers, the people who provide food, and all the other things." Everything is organized by the production people, who approach the shoot rather as an army general might. It is their job to map out the days, deciding which location will be used when, and then attempting to orchestrate each day so that it at least starts with some semblance of sense.

A considerable amount of planning has been done beforehand. Customs regulations insist that all items of clothing, down to cufflinks or tights, must be listed on a carnet, giving details of the material and the country of manufacture. The clothes are packed in the "Black Box" room in New

The preparations for the Cliveden shoot.

York, so called because the huge cases that can carry the clothes were originally black, although they are now gray. There might be as many as 40 of them, which means that the Lauren party must arrive at an airport at least two hours ahead of other passengers. But there has been a considerable amount of movement even before that. As Buffy Birrittella says, "There is always a major propping of locations. We never just walk in and start shooting." When they went to Hawaii for the Matisse shoot, four carpenters were sent down to construct a shack on the beach, which was pulled down at the end of the shoot. Then the crates of furniture and props arrive. Even at grand locations like Cliveden, changes are made: furniture is shipped in, bookcases built. The object is to create the fantasy dream and, for that, no trouble is too great. A loggia can be temporarily turned into a drawing room, complete with antique mirrors, precious rugs, crystal chandeliers, furniture, dogs on sofas, newspapers on the floor, writing materials on an escritoire— all where, previously, there had been nothing more than garden furniture and potted plants.

Because "things always happen on location," all clothes are unpacked the day before and everything goes out to the site. For the Cliveden shoot, that meant making a sizable selection from the 237 pairs of socks, 117 scarves and 321 ties brought from New York. Pressing begins at dawn. Local tailors are standing by, ready to alter clothes. As Pat Christman says, "They barely sleep for the next three days!" Everything must be ready and perfect for Bruce by 9.30 to 10.00 a.m. As male models dress much more quickly than female ones, who need hair and make-up, the day almost always begins with them.

"Bruce is a very instinctive photographer," Pat says. "He's very flexible, so he wants all the models there, all dressed ready for any exigencies. It could be as many as 30 models, all waiting, ready, for up to three days." This means that a wake-up call at five in the morning is no out-of-the-way thing. It takes time to transport models to a location, get them made up and dressed, ready to be called if Bruce wants them. The object of every day's shooting is to capture the dream with the sort of reality that will help the viewer enter into it. Nothing is posed, everything is extempore. There is always a certain amount of tension because everyone is conscious that, behind the images, they are searching for something almost ethereal, something that cannot be talked into tangible form in advance. It is a game of opportunism, of catching the fleeting, unrehearsed, and unexpected moment. The days are draining because they demand a high level of concentration and emotional involvement from all the principal players. The similarities with shooting a film are clear, but telling a story in pictures is much more difficult. Not only is there no script to act as an armature on which to construct each day's events, but all movements and gestures are eventually frozen so that any attempt at "acting" would result in an appearance of theatricality. That this does not happen is testimony to Bruce Weber's concentrated approach, which enables moments of inspired unexpectedness to occur. At all times, what he aims for is a naturalness which will enable models to relax, largely forget the camera, and behave not only in character with the clothes but also with their own personalities.

Each shoot has a storyboard, but it is of the loosest kind. Models are told simple identifying stories such as, "John, you and Chris went to college together and your girlfriend is Sophia." They will then play those characters for the four or five days of that particular shoot, each change of clothing or location acting as a scene in a movie would. The models relax and enjoy themselves, which is one of the advantages of using people who have worked together on previous Ralph Lauren shoots and know each other very well. As Pat says, "When you travel together a lot, you become a tightly bonded family." Even so, the Weber technique is both more wary and more subtle than this would suggest. He "builds" his story as he goes along and insists that everyone is dressed for the entire day, even if they are not officially expected to be shot. In this way the unplanned moments that usually make the best pictures can be captured. As Pat Christman explains, "Some of our best pictures have happened because people have been dressed and are hanging around doing what people do when they are not 'on stage'. That's when they are at their most natural, especially if they are kids. Bruce has eyes in the back of his head, even when he is shooting. Suddenly, he'll point and say, 'Oh, my God! Look at that!' and he'll go over and start shooting something which is happening naturally, not posed or anything. Or somebody will draw his attention to something, like 'Bruce, do you see Tom and Isabel talking over there by the tree?' and he'll go over and get the most wonderful picture." Ralph Lauren's open approach gives rise to this freedom to respond to the moment and follow a mood which is appropriate, but everyone is conscious that the object is to return with what he wants and expects, no matter how vaguely outlined. Although they know they have a considerable measure of creative freedom, no one forgets what Ralph usually tells them: "I don't want you to think that you can't go beyond but please remember what you've gone out to get."

Above: Ralph breaks with tradition— Tyson was part of many successful advertising campaigns.

The formula for print shoots was never actually stated, according to Buffy Birrittella. "It just evolved," she claims. "But, always, we are making a movie. Ralph's movie. It does not have a script but it does have a plot. It is always about the clothes and how people wearing them live." In order to release the chemistry between clothes, people, and atmosphere, locations are carefully chosen. They have included Paris, Ireland, and many parts of America, but perhaps the two most successful were the one which has become known as the Cliveden campaign, shot in England in 1987, and, in 1982, the print campaign of the safari collection shot in Hawaii. Both are classic examples of the power of the Ralph Lauren ethos to create images of lasting value and beauty. Were they not linked with advertising, Weber's images would be hailed as minor masterpieces of the art of photography.

It was decided to shoot the Cliveden campaign in England because the clothes were sophisticated and luxurious in the way that Ralph refers to as "Duchess of Windsor"—or, in Buffy's words, "grown-up, custom tailored, and luxurious." As the collection contained flannel suits and cashmere, everyone felt that the best place to shoot it to bring out its quality was England. As there were also many tweeds, Ralph wanted the shoot to have what Buffy calls "a city-country" feel. In conjunction with the English travel agents Terry and Chris Lawrence, who have organized many shoots for Ralph Lauren, it was decided to shoot in two locations: Eaton Square and Cliveden, once the home of the Astors but by that time a hotel. "We stayed in the Dorchester when we were in London," Buffy recalls. "But we took over Cliveden in its entirety. We wanted to be able to shoot throughout the whole house and to do so with guests would have been impossible. We were able to shoot in Nancy Astor's bedroom, on the balcony, and all that sort of thing. It was expensive—44 people were involved, of whom 20 were flown over from the States— but it actually worked out cheaper than staying in another hotel and renting different locations. We saved on a caterer by eating in the hotel dining room. In London, the Dorchester was fine for us because it had a service entrance at the back but we took over the Savoy lobby to shoot the party scene, and brought in gaming tables and lights especially for the day."

"Ralph is a nurturer of people. He gives them their freedom. It's part of his creative honesty."

Left: Spring 1984.

For the Safari shoot, it was decided to rule out Africa as Bruce Weber had shot there in the late seventies and his experiences convinced the Lauren organization that the logistical problems and the possibility of illness were too great. The challenge to the Lawrences was to find somewhere that would look like Africa. The surprising solution was the main island of Hawaii which, Buffy points out, has a terrain very similar to that of Kenya. "We shot on a private ranch and what we liked was the feeling of vastness in the landscape, there were even thica trees." She had decided that, to simulate the feeling of Africa, it was essential to have animals. Specifically, she wanted a zebra and some lion cubs. They had to be real, not stuffed. Even before anyone had thought of where they might come from, it was discovered that taking live animals into the state of Hawaii was extremely complex, if not entirely banned. After a great deal of negotiation it was agreed that animals could be brought in, provided they were kept in strict quarantine on the ranch, so that they could not come into contact with indigenous wildlife. A state wildlife official was to be present for the length of the shoot.

"The next question was the animals. Where were we going to get the animals?" Buffy laughs. "Chris Lawrence told me that he couldn't find any lion cubs because it was the wrong time of the year. Lions only breeding at a certain point, all the cubs he had found were already too big to be safely handled. I was thinking, 'Oh, God! This is crazy!' but I was determined not to give in. Luckily, the father of my boyfriend at that time was a good friend of the actress Tippi Hedren, and she had a ranch in California. By luck, it was a sort of Born Free place and she raised lions. She let us have three lion cubs and one ten-month-old lion, which was almost full-grown. But I still needed that zebra!" Just as she was beginning to despair, Tippi Hedren found one. Buffy's joy was shortlived. Chris Lawrence phoned to say that it was not possible to fly it to Hawaii in a cage. It would require a cargo plane and that would cost $22,000. "I remember saying to him, 'Chris, I have to do this photo.' He bargained with Pan Am and they came down to a reasonable price."

In addition to animals, personnel, and luggage have to be flown to locations. They normally travel on a scheduled flight, although special arrangements are made in advance so that the party does not arrive at the airport without warning with suitcases of clothes. The excess baggage charges are high because Buffy insists that everything that might be needed for a shoot is packed. Pat Christman remembers a shoot in Ireland where 300 ties were taken and the menswear stylists chose three, saying, "This is what Ralph is focused on. You can put the others away."

The complexities of a fashion shoot do not begin and end with transport. The Lauren shoots are multilayered affairs involving carpenters, builders, and upholsterers. Tents and beach umbrellas are specially made in the fabrics and colors required by the art directors who plan the sets. For a shoot in Santa Barbara in 1991, a tented house was created on the beach. The "potting shed" at the Lauren home in Bedford, a large, empty building with a dirt floor, has been paved and furnished to shoot a home collection. Ralph's tepee in Colorado has been used for the same purpose. If boats are required, they are hired: one for the models and one "chase" boat containing Bruce Weber and the stylist. People have walkie-talkie sets for communications. Clothes and personnel are transported in large mobile-home-type trailers, tents are set up for canteens, other tents shelter the clothes hung up in their hundreds. When a shoot has been in a place where the public has access it is not unknown for people, thinking it is a huge outdoor market, to ask the price of certain items. Like the vast traveling roadshow it is, everything has to be locked up and guarded at night, tents being re-erected next morning at dawn.

Overleaf: Spring 1984.

Getting it right on the battlefield could earn you a knighthood and Ralph has been getting it right creatively since the very beginning.

All the hard work seems worth it when, back in New York, the pictures come in. Bruce Weber does virtually no pre-selection, sending in hundreds of images for Ralph and his team to make their choice; Mario Testino, on the other hand, might choose four. One of the ways in which Ralph Lauren demonstrates confidence in both himself and his staff is in his ability to delegate in such matters. Having talked to his team and had a long conversation with Bruce he is sufficiently assured and relaxed not to meddle but to wait until he sees the pictures. As Buffy explains, "Both Bruce and I feel we have Ralph's confidence, and that gives us confidence in ourselves to be able to take what he has said and carry it forward. We know that if something happens which makes us see something new we go ahead just as if Ralph was there. We try to maintain the vision but we know Ralph has given us the freedom to take advantage of something inspirational happening." With the vast investment in time and money such an approach requires, it might seem from the outside that pinning things down more tightly before the team departs for a shoot could save both but, as Charles Fagan, president of Polo Retail Corporation, points out, "Ralph trusts his instincts and encourages others to do the same." It would simply not occur to him to take any other creative approach, although it can, very occasionally, lead to disappointment. At heart, Fagan believes, "Ralph is a nurturer of people. He gives them their freedom. It's part of his creative honesty." He adds, however, "He's also an enthusiast for hard work. As he once said to me, 'You'll always be moving uphill, if you're any good. Don't ever expect to be cruising downhill. When that happens, it's over.'"

Fashion shoots are expensive, so there is naturally some anxiety on the day when Ralph first comes in to see the pictures. Carter, only half-joking, says, "You're sitting at the table with him and when he starts to look through them, you're metaphorically clutching your hair, saying "Please, God, let him like them." Of course, there are times when he is disappointed. And I always know. He is sifting through the pictures and there's no reaction. I'm thinking, Oh no. He's looking for something and he hasn't found it. Then he'll say, 'Okay. Let's see something else.' We're all dying— not because of the huge costs but because we've failed him. But he is always so generous in these situations, he'll say, 'You know what? I know you did exactly what I asked you to but it doesn't look right to me now. I'm not blaming you. I was part of this. Let's see how we can make this work.'"

Lauren will keep sifting through the pictures until he finds one or two that work. The team goes back to the archives, pulling out pictures with the right spirit until finally the story emerges. As Pat Christman says, "He always comes up with something that can save the situation." Carter points out that, even when Ralph is not entirely sure of the results, his team is so attuned to his thinking that, more often than not, they hit close enough to the target for him to be able to make the images work. "He will say, 'I like that color,' or 'I don't like this,' and all the time he's setting up signposts for us. He uses film as a reference, of course. He thinks cinematically. His tradition is Hollywood. In order to keep abreast I have to go to Blockbuster video to get the films he talks about. Almost always he is able to save the day. And I'm always so relieved. You see, what is remarkable about the man is his trust. He really trusts his team. He sends us out and trusts us to bring it back. He would never insult us by coming out to keep a check." And it is because he trusts and likes them that Ralph Lauren tries to find a creative solution, to produce something that will not leave them feeling that they have let him down. As Carter says, "Ralph always likes a happy ending."

The dream world created for a print advertising campaign is heightened when it becomes film, a medium Ralph Lauren has used most successfully for his perfumes and, more recently, Polo.com. Commercials which, even more than Safari, are archetypal. As Buffy Birritella explains, "the Polo.com ads are broad-based, whereas a campaign like Safari was specific, they capture the entire Ralph Lauren world from the runway to the playing field. Polo.com is a major branding vehicle for Polo Ralph Lauren. Those sixty-second ads really capture the Ralph Lauren world." All Lauren fragrances mix the traditional with the modern, as the clothes do, and the result is often an instant modern classic. For example, the cut-crystal bottle for Lauren, sealed with a gold cover, is part of the permanent collection of the Cooper Hewitt Museum. One of the most successful perfume campaigns was for Safari. As is appropriate for a name that comes from the African word for "bon voyage," it was decided that the right degree of exotic adventure intended to be conjured by the name could only be found on location in Africa. Ralph and Buffy both felt strongly that, although the print campaign in Hawaii had worked well, television needed the real thing. They wanted the light and atmosphere of east Africa and the genuine color of Kenya in order to reconstruct the imaginative quality of Hemingway's *The Snows of Kilimanjaro* or the book *Out of Africa* by Isak Dinesen. Filming was complex. A small village of over 50 tents was erected on site for the crew. Props, furnishings, and extras were flown in. The "star" was model Kim Nye, whose wardrobe was especially created for the film. Along with the whole crew, she was guarded by Masaai, hired especially on site. Les Goldberg directed and Renato Berta, who had worked together on Louis Malle's film *Au Revoir les Enfants*, was director of photography.

It could be said that, given the right people, it is not too difficult to capture the imagination of viewers with a short, evocative television campaign linked to a name already associated with glamour and the class of high-quality WASP clothing, but the world of lifestyle encompasses other areas with which it is generally considered harder to engage the public imagination. In the case of Ralph Lauren, the charisma of the name seems to disarm any resistance. Polo home furnishings are an excellent example. Before Ralph Lauren, the top end of "fashion for the home" was looked after by the interior decorators, of whom America had produced some of the world's finest, going back to Edith Wharton and her ground-breaking work on the aesthetics of decorating the home, and including such names as Billy Baldwin and, above all, Sister Parrish, the woman whose decorative tradition Ralph Lauren can be said to be continuing. He recalls that, when he first decided in the early eighties that home furnishings were the next logical move in his design cannon, many of his admirers were appalled. "They said, 'You're not going to do sheets and things like that!' He laughs. They reacted as if it was a sell out."

Initially, problems were expected. As the magazine Home Fashions Textiles pointed out in June 1983, "The name game in home furnishings has never been played as expertly or taken quite as seriously [in the interior decorating field] as it has been on Seventh Avenue." Lauren himself realized that he was working in a different world, as he acknowledged: "The consumer will never say, as they might with my clothing lines, 'That's a Ralph Lauren. I'll buy it.' The product alone will make it sell." In this, Lauren was being disingenuous. His advertising campaigns for home furnishings, shot in the main by Bruce Weber, were entirely of a type with the advertising campaigns for other Lauren products. The product was strong, but the brand name more than

Right: The range of products in Ralph Lauren Home extends to include paint.

matched it. He also knew—again, as with his clothing lines—that the range and amount of product was crucial in gaining his target audience. As he said when he launched home furnishings, he had often been asked "to do a designer sheet. I mean, what's a sheet? What does it mean? What I design is more environmental. A mood." Buffy Birrittella explains, "Ralph was the first designer to take his whole design concept from apparel into a full-blown home collection. Remember, we didn't just do tablewear or sheets or bathwear, we also did lifestyles within those categories, so that there would be, say, a Thoroughbred collection or a Jamaica collection. It was—right from the beginning—part of Ralph's desire to celebrate the roots of his country: New England, the American West, the northern woodsman, the fisherman on the keys of Florida." In Ralph's words, "I designed everything I loved. I put together all the worlds as if I were going out to buy for my own home."

Since his first homewear collection in 1983, the driving force behind the Ralph Lauren approach to furnishings has been twofold: to celebrate a certain history, especially that of America, and to reflect his own needs and wishes. As he told *Elle Decor* in 1993, "I have different houses and I want to live differently in each. In the city I might want a sophisticated look… but in the country it might be nice to have a little pattern or something like old washed-out chambray." It has proved a winning formula, incorporating the sort of flexibility that Ralph Lauren likes. His approach was unique back in 1983. Nobody had seen the potential in breaking out of set categories such as bedding, wall coverings, linen, or fabrics and marketing them together as a themed approach. The broad theme characterizations, in addition to Thoroughbred and Jamaica, were Log Cabin and New England, and so right were they for the Lauren ethos that his furnishings still work within those categories. "I don't go with the hot mood of the moment," he explains. "I go with things that have longevity, that I think are going to last for ever. My challenge is to make the timeless modern and exciting… my personal taste has always been eclectic."

In order to ensure that his approach is understood, twice a year Lauren presents his new product line in room sets created on his thematic approach: In addition to the original four, the categories have included Safari, Sante Fe, Mercer Street, and Irish Coast. The sets are remarkably lifelike. They do not include Lauren products alone. The personality of the imagined owner is evoked by the choice of books and pictures, the flowers and framed photographs. A pair of gloves or a tennis racket might be left lying around. Even the choice of fruit in a bowl is significant in order to create an environment which is not only a total but also a personal experience. Lauren sells home products as he sells his clothing line—by telling a story so carefully that it is totally convincing. As he says, "People have to be shown a way of living." Nowadays, he does this through the medium of Alfredo Parades, executive vice president, Creative Services, Polo Store Development and Home Collection Design Studio. "It's my job to image Ralph," he says. "And I think I know how to do it. I've been with him since 1986 when I first came out of college and I started in display at the Mansion, the Polo Ralph Lauren flagship store on Madison Avenue. He nurtured my taste and now I help flesh out his ideas. I know how he thinks. He'll say something like, 'I want to feel barefoot. It's Jamaica and I want to feel how you feel when you get out of the shower. White tennis shorts. It's six o'clock. What do you want the place to feel like?' Then I throw things out at him and he'll say, 'Yes, I love that. I don't like that.' It involves a lot of honesty and trust, but it's an approach we have evolved and it really works."

INTERIOR SEMI-GLOSS

PAINT

RALPH LAUREN

PREMIUM QUALITY 100% ACRYLIC

DESIGN STUDIO WHITE

RL 13015

ONE GALLON (3.78 liters)

"Ralph was the first designer to take his whole design concept from apparel into a full-blown home collection."

Above: Modern living and urban sophistication.

Parades points out that one of the special things about working with Ralph Lauren is that everyone is working within one aesthetic, which is constantly evolving. He believes that Lauren's success is a reflection of the fact that, even when he is at his most contemporary, there is always the seed of a future classic in what he does. "He's never so edgy that he's so completely of the moment that, next year, it's dead. It's about taste—and I really can't think of any designer who has such a broad appreciation of different approaches to living." The Home Collection design studio is split into four divisions: bed and bath; furniture; decorative accessories, which includes lighting, carpeting, home fragrance, and tablewear; and fabric by the yard, which is, according to Parades, "a huge business."

The range of products is considerable. Ralph Lauren paint, for example, shows the extent and subtlety of the Lauren organization's thinking, in its determination not only to sell to the widest audience but also to develop the response of that audience to the product. At its launch in 1996, Lauren was the first designer to put his name to a paint and wallcovering line. For that reason, it had to be sold not as a utilitarian product but as something as alluring and upmarket as every other item bearing the Polo name. This was achieved in the traditional Lauren manner—by superb photography. Advertising campaigns featured the paint tin, which had as its label the Stars and Stripes. Colors were grouped generically: Thoroughbred, Santa Fe; Thoroughbred, Southport. Advertisements claimed, "68 Perfect Shades of White," with names such as polo-mallet white, tuxedo shirt, pocket-watch white, and Edwardian linen. The copy was vintage Polo Ralph Lauren, evocative and enticing: "From the Ralph Lauren paint collection, the subtle nuances of light and density, capable of capturing every texture, every form, every mood… the colors of America, bringing spirit and character to the home." Its mood was uncannily akin to Lauren's advertisements for his clothing in the mid-eighties: "To feel the pleasure of knowing that what you are wearing has been tailored to become a respected member of your wardrobe, maintaining its integrity with time…."

If the advertisements suggest an immutability in Polo as product, Ralph Lauren as businessman has never failed to look forward. Always interested in partnerships that would enhance the status of the firm and increase capital for development and investment, in the early nineties he was planning where to take the firm for the next decade and beyond. At the same time, Edgar Bronfman, the chief operating officer of Seagrams, was considering making a move into "high-end consumer goods." Bronfman recalls, "We actually talked about the possibility of his selling the business. I was interested because I was toying with the idea of creating an American version of LVMH. We made Ralph a very substantial offer but he had a firm sense of the value of his company which, based on numbers, was not warranted but he was convinced of the soundness of his company in the future and he rejected it. I admired the way he stuck to his guns. He had a very strong sense of the worth of what he had created." Bronfman's plan was predicated on Lauren maintaining creative control—"There would be no point in owning a company called Ralph Lauren without Ralph"—but shortly after the deal fell through Polo Ralph Lauren did a deal with Goldman Sacks. On June 12, 1997, Polo became a publicly traded company on the New York stock exchange, with Ralph Lauren as its chief executive officer.

Bronfman believes that Ralph was ambivalent about whether to stay private or go public and, as they had become good friends, he felt he should warn him against it. "It's no fun running a public company, especially for someone like Ralph, who is really a creator and an essentially

Above left and right: Room settings for contemporary furnishings.

instinctive person. Quarterly reports to shareholders are not consistent with that atmosphere and world. But I think he wanted a public validation of what he had built—and, of course, its worth." To Bronfman it was the inevitable next move in the Lauren cycle, but he regretted it on Ralph's behalf because he knew Ralph had built something so special, based on his instinctive feelings, with no need to justify any decision to anybody else, that it could not help but be affected by the new situation. "Shareholders want results," he says. "One of the ways they get them is by cutting back on budgets. Ralph's creativity has always been expensive but it is at the core of his business. He needs freedom. Ralph Laurens come along only very rarely."

Lauren wears his public face well. If he is conscious of what Bronfman sees as a vital shift of gravity in his company, none but his most intimate advisers will ever be aware of it. In his 1999 report to shareholders, he wrote "I see a brand that, for over three decades, has spoken to the world with a visual vocabulary that articulates style, quality, and an original vision of American values and traditions. That brand is now a global business that transcends fashion, earning us millions of consumers in over 60 countries, who have woven the Polo lifestyle into their daily lives. I see a company that is proud of its achievements, driven to succeed by consistently combining innovative thinking and business acumen. I see tremendous growth potential ahead…." It was a declaration of faith in the past and the ability to deliver in the future. In the report for 2000, Ralph took it further and clearly stated the rationale at the core of his tremendous success: "At Polo Ralph Lauren, style is much more than the cut of a lapel or the richness of a color. It's the embodiment of who you are—at home, at work, at play. Your likes, your passions, your values. That is not something that changes week to week. It stays with you for a lifetime." To clinch his point, he added that Polo brands had generated $4.5 billion in wholesale sales in the previous year.

In February 2000 Ralph Lauren took a step he had been pondering for several years. Acutely aware of the selling potential of the new media, he and his son David had thoroughly researched the possibility offered by the Internet. Ralph decided to launch Polo.com which, as the press handout explained, is "a destination site dedicated to the American lifestyle, that will include original content, commerce, and a strong community component." It was a joint venture with NBC and was aimed at "targeting a broad demographic" shared by both companies. David Lauren was made director and vice president of marketing for Ralph Lauren Media. As always, Ralph's winning way with words was in evidence at the press conference. "What I've been doing is about living," he said. "How do you spend your leisure time—and what do you wear to do those things. The connection here is a new future; a new world of entertainment, information, and excitement. I'm challenged to take my company further. The new media gives us the ability to launch a new concept. But I still think stores are important. I don't think anything is outmoded."

Polo.com is the latest in a string of "firsts" with which Ralph Lauren has activated and moved forward both the fashion business and retailing over the past 35 years. A born leader, he has been so closely followed in both fields that his attitudes are all-pervasive. There is not a store that does not reflect his thinking about retail. There is not an advertising campaign that does not reveal the influence of a Bruce Weber shoot for Ralph Lauren. As Rob Frieda says, "Ralph showed everybody else how to do it. He gave them the road map to follow—and they're still following. He is the true aristocrat of his world."

making it happen

If Ralph Lauren sometimes gives the impression of being preoccupied, it is not surprising. He is titular head of a considerable empire that encompasses wholesale and retail businesses, all of which require his time to a greater or lesser degree. In addition, the Polo Ralph Lauren business, which has a revenue of well over $2 billion per year, now includes a wide range of licensees.

Wholesale operations for Lauren's men's and women's dress fall into Collection brands and Polo brands, their design, sourcing, marketing and distribution. The Collection brands are Purple Label for men and Collection and Black Label for women. These represent the pinnacle of the pyramid, the crème de la crème of the Ralph Lauren world: exclusive, expensive, using the finest materials garnered from around the world, made by the best tailors and dressmakers in Europe and America—Purple Label has been made by traditional craftsmen in England but is now manufactured in Italy—these ranges set the benchmark of excellence for everything else produced by Ralph Lauren. On a slightly lower level, produced for a different price point, the Polo brands group includes Polo Ralph Lauren for men, Polo Dress Furnishings, which encompasses all accessories, Polo Sport for Men and Polo Golf. The women's ranges are Ralph Lauren Blue Label and Ralph Lauren Golf, which also includes a range for men. The company's retail operations are split into two separate but complementary groups covering full-price and outlet stores. At full-price level, the Polo Ralph Lauren stores across America and the world are the public retail face of the world of Ralph Lauren, involved with promulgating lifestyle attitudes as much as selling clothes and home collection items.

650 Madison is a perfect symbol of Ralph Lauren, being as quixotic and as paradoxical as he himself can be …

An identical role is played by the Polo Sport stores, which stock active sportswear and casual clothing. Also part of the retail section, but at an appreciably lower price level, Polo Jeans, aimed at a younger aspirational market. In May 1999 when Polo Ralph Lauren acquired the Canadian-based retailer Club Monaco, which offers a modern, clean look for men and women at a price. In addition, the outlet store group includes Polo Ralph Lauren full-line factory stores, alongside concept factory stores such as Lauren and Polo Jeans Co. Ralph Lauren products are also sold in top-quality department and specialty stores throughout the world. It was Ralph Lauren's 1971 arrangement with Bloomingdale's to give him his own shop-in-shop boutique in their New York flagship store that led to the situation we know today, whereby instore boutiques are a common feature of the better stores in virtually every country across the globe.

The empire reaches further, designing and producing items for sixteen product licensing partners, eleven Home Collection licensing partners, and twelve international licensing partners. They include, for example, in clothing product licensees, Lauren by Ralph Lauren and Chaps Ralph Lauren manufactured by Peerless Clothing International, with the women's range being the responsibility of the Jones Apparel Group, which also produce the RALPH range. Polo by Ralph Lauren is made in Italy by Corneliani and Ralph Lauren's childrenswear is the responsibility of the S.chwab company. International licensees include Reebok, L'Oreal, and Warnaco. In the home collection, towels, sheets and bedding are made by Westpoint Stevens, paint by ICI Glidden, and furniture by Henredon Furniture Industries, Inc.

The company nerve center, where Ralph has his office, is at 650 Madison Avenue, although the empire's outposts include not only other New York addresses, such as 980 Madison Avenue and 550 Seventh Avenue, but also further locations in New Jersey, Florida and Texas. The internal telephone directory, published annually, lists more than 1,500 telephone numbers in its A-Z of personnel, in addition to the 96 corporate officers who run the gamut from Ralph himself, through the vice chairman, Lance Isham, to Roger Farah, president and chief operating officer of Polo Ralph Lauren and Bridget Ryan Berman, president and chief operating officer of Polo Retail Concepts.

The offices at 650 Madison are a perfect symbol for Ralph Lauren, being as quixotic and as paradoxical as he himself can be. They exemplify the dichotomy in his creative and artistic thinking, being both traditional and modern at one and the same time. The building in which the Lauren headquarters are situated is a glass and steel monument to necessity, with no distinguishing features to lighten its predictability. The visitor passes through swing doors set in a wall of glass to enter a vast area lined and floored in gray marble, containing nothing but a reception center, set well back with an elevator block behind it. So far, so anonymous. None of this was designed by Ralph Lauren, of course. It is the standard lobby area found in a thousand expensive examples of business real estate scattered across the commercial centers of North America. To experience the world of Ralph Lauren it is necessary to take the elevator to the sixth floor, where visitors instantly enter a distinct world, but one familiar to anyone who has visited any of Ralph Lauren's retail outlets.

The rich, dark-paneled lift area is dominated by a plinth on which stands a bronze of the Ralph Lauren polo player. In the reception area the full impact of the atmosphere strikes home. This is Lauren-land, warm, accommodating, slightly overwhelming, and offering a subtle mixture of design antecedents. The warmth of the paneling is reminiscent of turn-of-the-century mansions; the chairs, deep and comfortable, and the tables, piled high with illustrated books, remind one of luxury hotels or ocean-going liners from the same period. The atmosphere is gracious, calm, and still. Paintings include portraits, pictures of horses, and one 6-foot-long street scene of late-Victorian businessmen which seems especially appropriate in that the men are impeccably dressed and exude social assurance. Just when it all seems just a little too atavistic to avoid pomposity, the eye notices a large Sterling silver bowl full to the brim with multicolored M&Ms, from which everyone who passes scoops a handful.

Walking along the corridor to Ralph's office and those belonging to the members of the Polo staff who need to be near him could be a sombre experience were not the darkly paneled walls, on which one would normally expect to see hung heavy Victorian pictures in deep gilt frames, lightened by large black-and-white photographs from Weber publicity campaigns, framed to accentuate rather than diminish their modernity. Such frissons abound: old club leather is offset by zebra skin; an Edwardian table is dressed not with a volume on Currier and Ives or a gold-tooled period volume but a starkly black-and-white book of photographs of downtown lofts.

The mix is visually successful because it manifests a very self-conscious and contrived approach to interior decorating, starting from the modern interior decorator's view—how will this space, vista, or angle photograph? Every vignette catching the eye does so in the way in which the eye would be caught by a picture in an interior-decorating book or magazine. It says much about the sensibility that Lauren has created over the years in every area of his world and developed in virtually everyone who works with him in that world. The result is uncannily like looking at a series of pictures in a magazine. The style is essentially in-house. Although the headquarters were designed by an outside design firm, Shelton, Mendel, and Associates, all the decoration, which includes the furniture, art, books, and accessories, was the responsibility of the Polo design committee led by Buffy Birrittella, Nancy Vignola—in 1992, when Polo Ralph Lauren moved to the new headquarters, the senior vice president of Home Collection design and Creative Services—and Jeff Walker, vice president of Creative Services, who died shortly before the move into the new premises. Together, they brought to bear the corporate eye that they and Ralph have spent so many years developing.

The mood in the public areas, including a magnificent mahogany staircase that sweeps from top to bottom of four of the eight-floor empire and which required over a year to be carved and created, is luxurious, grand even, but its formality never becomes stuffy. In a strange way, it is the perfect background for the fit and toned youthful employees who cross and crisscross the elegant spaces throughout the day. The lasting effect is one of class as seen through Hollywood eyes. Although its romantic cocoon makes it easy to assume that it is a showcase and nothing more, 650 Madison works with total efficiency.

Imagining otherwise is a trap into which the casual visitor might fall, but anyone whose business takes him behind the public facade would see the other side of 650 Madison, the side where the daily work goes on. Here there is more wood but this time it is light maple, which calmly contrasts with the black-and-white-squared floors which, in turn, contrast with the wooden floors that look as if they could be in a state-of-the-art modern gymnasium. The walls are white. There is a co-ed college mood to the reference library and workstations, heightened by the fact that, as elsewhere, there is no dress code for the staff. As long as it is clean, stylish, and young, staff of both sexes can dress down on every day of the week—but it has to be said that the jeans are always fashionably cut. Like the surroundings themselves, the only criterion for the staff is style.

At the center of all this is Ralph Lauren's office, surely the most idiosyncratic and personal space ever created by the chairman and CEO of a multibillion dollar international business. Within this modest space can be found everything that has ever mattered to Ralph Lauren. Eschewing the vast and intimidatingly empty aircraft hangar-like offices favored by many of his counterparts, Ralph has taken a small room and created his own den. Its informality reflects the mood of the whole headquarters, shown even in how Ralph dresses to come to work. He chooses his wardrobe not as others may think suitable to his position but to reflect his mood of the moment. He might be wearing a Purple Label Prince of Wales check suit but he's much more likely to be in a faded and frayed denim shirt, jeans, a silver-tipped leather belt, and hand-tooled cowboy boots, or a black T-shirt, combat pants and Navaho beads at his neck.

Left: Creative clutter in Ralph's office.

The atmosphere is a good one and can perhaps more justifiably be described as "family" here than in most fashion empires. No one, for example, ever calls Ralph Mr. Lauren. It cannot be coincidental that many of the staff, from Audrey Schilt and Alistaire McRobbie, his long-term creative designers for womenswear, to vice president of corporate archives Pat Christman and Buffy herself, have been with the organization for many years.

The people who come to work for Ralph Lauren tend to stay, not only because they become committed to his vision but also because there is a feeling of accessibility at all levels of the organization, and they feel that their voice carries some weight. And they are right. Consultation is a bedrock of the firm. Ralph Lauren canvasses opinions on all levels, soliciting the views of his staff in an informal way. He has been known to leave a gridlocked meeting, taking with him swatches of fabric, garments, or accessories over which stalemate has been reached, and walk down the corridor to the main reception area soliciting the opinions of whomever he meets. It's the technique Ralph Lauren uses with his planning committees and with his design teams. He wants to know what everybody thinks and if they fail to make themselves clear initially, he'll ask questions until they do. Everybody is proud of their entitlement to add a little to the creative process—but no one who works for Ralph Lauren is under any misapprehension. This is not design by committee. Ralph listens, takes all views on board, and then makes his own decision. There are some in the organization who feel that he has done that long before the casual, impromptu consultations take place and that he uses them to reinforce his views. Be that as it may, the working area of the Ralph Lauren corporate headquarters makes such social and business interchanges easy. Much of the area is open plan, broken up into workstations, and even when there are office doors, they are, including Ralph's, closed only rarely and even then more for the need to concentrate and be undisturbed than for a desire for privacy, let alone secrecy.

This means there is nothing awe-inspiring about Ralph's office, what one sees jumbled together on the walls, covering his desk, and piled up on the floor is the man and the life. The basic furnishings are simple: leather armchairs, white sofa, glass-topped table. They are overwhelmed by a tidal wave of objects gifts from family, staff and friends or accumulated by Ralph over the years which express his eclectic and childlike spirit. Black-and-white photographs of cowboys, vintage cars, and movie stars are stacked four or five deep against the walls, along with framed art-deco posters. More black-and-white photographs on the walls sit next to early primitive paintings,

above a vintage bicycle with an ancient saddle draped over it. There are toys and teddy bears everywhere. Tartan boxes, models of the world's classic car marques, and early nineteenth-century toys jostle with family pictures on the desk, which include a signed picture of Ralph with the Princess of Wales. Behind Ralph's seat is another signed photograph, from Frank Sinatra, one of his great heroes, saying "Thanks for your ties—they're smashing." Illustrated books are piled everywhere, their subjects ranging from Buggati, Aston Martin, and Ferrari to photographers, Avedon, Penn, Maplethorpe, and Horst prominent among them. From the ceiling hang model planes. The effect is of the sort of controlled visual chaos that builds up over many generations in a family house where nothing is ever destroyed, thrown away, or sold but things are frequently lost for centuries. It is a mix most people would find indigestible and eventually overwhelming but it sets the house style: the offices of other long-term Lauren employees have the same hotchpotch, higgledy-piggledy mix, including those of Buffy and Mary Randolph Carter, who play such a strong role in the advertising campaigns. It must be said that the effects are what interior designers and magazine editors spend long hours and considerable amounts of money trying to replicate.

No designing is done in Ralph's office. When fabrics have to be chosen or samples filtered and eliminated, he goes to the appropriate working area. Despite the plethora of things bearing the Polo Ralph Lauren label or logo that eventually reach the stores—and they run into the tens of thousands each season—none of the important items sold in the full-price retail market is passed without being seen, if not by Ralph or Buffy, then by someone senior whose eye can be trusted. Ralph Lauren's approach is hands-on and everyone who is responsible for no matter what design area tries hard to obtain his approbation and the benefit of his unerring taste, knowing that he has an unbeatable eye for color, scale, and proportion when it comes to creating the special Lauren visual mélange.

But is it a question of him being, as Cézanne said of Monet, "Only an eye, but what an eye," or can Ralph Lauren lay a great claim to the title of designer? The question exercises him even more than it intrigues the fashion world. Certainly, people are prepared to praise him, often extravagantly, for his many achievements. Lance Isham points out, "He not only has a vision, he's had a myriad of firsts. Pre-eminently, he was the first person to truly develop a lifestyle sensibility. In a sense, the company is an evolution of his life. Throughout all the struggles and difficulties— and there have been both—he maintained his vision, never forgetting where he came from nor where he was aiming to go. I think that's inspiring." One of Ralph's friends, who almost became a business partner, is Edgar Bronfman. As shrewd as he is worldly, he finds Ralph Lauren, "a great credit to America in that he has changed our culture. Certainly, he revolutionized America's visual aspirations," he claims. "He was the visual voice of America in the eighties and nineties, with Calvin Klein answering him—in a different tone—and the pretenders to the throne such as the Donna Karans and Tommy Hilfigers trying to emulate them both. But it was Ralph who created an entire lifestyle. He actually stands for something whereas Calvin is really just a recognizable name. Ralph wants to be known as a great designer. He really wants that recognition. He's always hungry for reinforcement but we must remember that the greatest creativity is borne out of insecurity. I know nobody who is wonderfully creative and gifted who is entirely secure. I think

... this is Ralph Lauren's office, surely the most idiosyncratic and personal space ever created by the chairman and CEO of a multibillion dollar business.

the two are mutually exclusive. Ralph's ambition is to be remembered. That is why he's upset when people refer to him as a great marketeer or lifestyle creator. He assumes it denigrates him. I suppose, above all, he wants affirmation from his peers. Nothing is ever enough for Ralph. He wants to live in history."

Other creators may be prepared to line up and praise, but that is often not enough. That is certainly the case with Ralph Lauren. As he was once heard to say after receiving an honor, "Everybody always says, 'You were great, Ralph,' but nobody ever says I am good." The people he feels say it least of all are the fashion press, after his customers the one group most important to him. This has been a long-running sore. "No one has to tell me if a collection is great," he says. "I know that. And, obviously, not every collection is so exciting. But I look for the sort of sincere criticism a good fashion editor should be able to give and I don't see it. Even 'Ralph, the collection was you,' is a sincere reaction, but I don't get that often, either. I'm proud of what I've achieved. I came from nowhere. I was a revolutionary. I took a moribund, struggling tie business and I changed everything. I put things together to make a whole look. I loved everything English. I took from the American heritage and I built up a modern look, piece by piece. I think the press never 'got' my work because it was always real. That's why I have always been copied. I find it very upsetting when the press say my work is derivative because it is based on American culture. They don't say that about designers in Paris who spend their time creating fancy-dress costumes. When I read some of the criticisms, I think, 'Have I been living in a vacuum for thirty-five years?' What comes out in my collections is me. It's my world. I've broken ground in what I've done." In an advertising campaign given as long ago as 1984, he explained the wellsprings of his design philosophy and how the cheap race for the latest headline-grabbing thing could never be him when he said, "There is a way of living that has a certain grace and beauty. It is not a constant race for what is next; rather, an appreciation of what has come before. There is a respect for quality, a recognition of what is truly meaningful. These are the feelings I would like my work to inspire. This is the quality of life that I believe in." It upsets him that what he feels is self-evident seems to be so often ignored by fashion commentators.

Although he feels he has a genuine grievance, Ralph Lauren has been—and still is—appreciated. The reviews of his Collection for spring/summer 2001, for example, included *Women's Wear Daily* hailing him as "pure, intriguing, and full of snap." *The New York Post* described him as scoring with "a clean, spare, and graphic collection"; while the *International Herald Tribune* noted, "With no references to the past or to American culture, Lauren served up clothes that seemed fresh and graphic, classy and refined...." A reading of past press cuttings confirms that Ralph Lauren's shows have almost always been mentioned favorably and only rarely denigrated. Even when journalists have not always been happy with a collection in its entirety, the variety within his shows has always produced at least one thing, and frequently more, for them to pinpoint and praise.

For the sort of overview expected of the editor of a fashion magazine, as opposed to the writing of a fashion journalist who might have only a limited knowledge of his or her subject, it is instructive to turn to one who was working when Ralph was just beginning. Grace Mirabella, who was editor of *American Vogue* throughout the seventies, has watched his career grow through three decades and finds his progress very interesting. "I first met him in the late sixties, when I was with *Vogue* as an associate of Diana Vreeland, the editor," she recalls. "Then I became editor in 1970, a

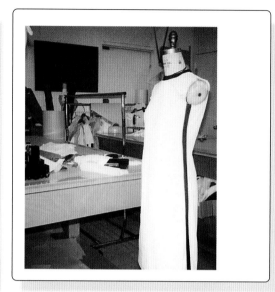

Above: Finalizing all the details for a fashion show.

time when there was a great surge forward in American sportswear, spearheaded by Ralph. What was wonderful was to watch him and his company grow, always moving from one office to another and getting bigger all the time. But what fascinated me about Ralph was his consistency— of style and image. In fact, what he is faulted for is what any other designer would relish having. I mean, what's so terribly wrong about having a real, developed style? He doesn't reinvent himself day by day. He moves forward inch by inch—and surely that is style? We're not talking dumb clothes here. We're talking about important clothes. Sadly, they don't always fit into the journalese of fashion, which is—and has to be—about change. But he was a standard-bearer. And he has talent where many others have merely got the games which designers can play to manipulate the media.

"He can take it, as well. I remember in the late seventies *Vogue* did a feature on the American collections and we did not give him great prominence because we really felt that it wasn't one of his best seasons and there were others that season which were more interesting. Anyhow, I got a phone call from Ralph. How could I do it? He became more and more angry. I just listened. I mean, what are you going to say? Finally, he stopped. There was a pause and I said, 'Ralph, listen. I know what you're saying but I want to say only one thing to you: I did not design the collection.' He laughed and said, 'Okay.' And that was the end of it. But normally he has the goods and they say, 'Hey! listen. Here's who I am and here's what I do.' He is a key American designer who creates a compelling style for a certain kind of woman. But what is really smart is how he has conveyed that style into every category of everything he does. That's why I'm a fan. I think it is very hard to do that – just as it is to keep consistency."

The work required to produce the Ralph Lauren womenswear collection every six months is considerable. It starts even before the previous collection has been shown, with various people in the design teams beginning to discuss ideas with Max X Wilson, vice president, women's collection design, he has been with Ralph for over ten years and is the person who will work most closely with Ralph and Buffy in the coming months. As Gerri Anderson, senior director of operations for women's design, says, "We may see Ralph twice a week, which is unheard of with most of the design teams, who only see him twice a month." The reason Ralph Lauren concentrates on women's Collection, in addition to Purple Label, is easily understood since these collections are the most fashion forward and inspire all other lines. Because the collection is viewed by the world's press at Ralph Lauren's fashion show, it is the thing that pre-eminently affects his status— and possibly sales for the next six months, although the Lauren customer is, like the supporters of most other top designers, remarkably faithful. It would have to be a very uninspired collection for her to look elsewhere.

In common with his fellows, Ralph finds the fashion show a form of crucifixion, and indeed it is. All designers have to wrestle with the fact that six months' work, considerable expense, and phenomenal man hours—in the run-up to a collection, thirteen-hour days, or longer, are far from exceptional—are seen and assessed in the brief space of twenty minutes. The fashion press, possibly jaded and tired from viewing other shows in the concentrated period of New York Fashion Week, have to make their assessment on the brief exposure and might have to file their copy so quickly after the show that all they can ever give is an instant and often superficial reaction to what they see.

And yet their copy is of vital importance. Designers know that the fashion press's words are read over breakfast, on commuter trains, and in coffee breaks the next morning and that is the only critical assessment they will receive. What potential customers learn then is almost always all that they will know of a collection until advertising campaigns, aimed much more at beguiling than informing, are produced by the fashion houses many months later, by which time design teams have already moved on and are beginning to create their ideas boards for the following season's collection. At Ralph Lauren, the boards contain sketches, color swatches, finished fashion illustrations, pages torn from magazines, reference books, and often examples of clothing from previous Ralph Lauren collections. A great deal of time and effort goes into the thinking behind these boards: Their job is to stimulate Ralph's imagination and give him a lead-in to his next collection. Like all designers, he comes to the preliminary meetings with his own ideas for the theme of the next collection already in his mind. Tentative, vague, and unfleshed—no specific colors, textures, or patterns—it is the spirit of a collection which the boards are meant to convey, by fitting in with what Ralph already has in the back of his mind. In fact, he often does not quite realize what is in the back of his mind until it is triggered off by something on a particular board which catches his eye. As Gerri Anderson says, "He comes in, listens to what the design teams say, spends a great deal of time examining the boards and then begins to pull out ideas."

"You know, Ralph," somebody says, picking up a silk scarf with a thirties' feel to it, "We're thinking sort of this way with colors." He'll pick it up, look at it, and listen to further explanations, but no hasty decisions are made this early. However, the colors—and perhaps the textures—have been lodged in the collective memory bank. Someone produces a polaroid: "I wonder, should we be thinking very clean 'spectator' at this point? Maybe a little south of France…." Nothing is too remote or unlikely. One season, the design team was inspired by the sleek red of Ralph's collection of Ferraris but the stimulus could be something as apparently anonymous as how a basket has been woven. As always, it is Ralph's responses that carry the process forward.

At this stage, most of the talking is done by Max X Wilson, who guides Ralph through his design team's thinking. On hand are fabric specialists and one of the creative team responsible for interpreting Ralph's ideas through their sketches. If an idea catches his imagination, he will turn and say, "Do me a sketch of that, will you?" Within the space of two minutes he has it. Apart from Max and Ralph, everybody in the room is taking notes. Buffy watches Ralph closely, interpreting his body language, noticing his eyes. He is filtering everything he is shown through his own ideas for the season's look. Someone points out something on the board. Ralph reacts quickly. "I love it but not for now. It's wrong for this time. But it's a great concept. Let's hold it. Maybe it would do for Cruise." This is a mild way of saying that he doesn't think the concept is wrong but feels that it is not strong enough for the main collection, Cruise being a transition collection that hits stores at holiday time. It may be a knock backward for the design team but they accept it.

The team lead Ralph through everything they have pinned on the boards or laid out on tables. As the meeting moves on and he warms up, he becomes more vocal and positive. By the time he leaves the meeting, the design team has a focused idea of how he is thinking, although little if anything has been firmly decided. Ringing in everybody's ears are the words that invariably terminate these meetings. As he walks for the door, Ralph says, "I need more." Everybody knows it and, by the time he comes to the next meeting, the team will have built on what he has chosen. The concept is broadened by the introduction of more pieces and the process continues until

Ralph feels he has the beginning of what will be the new line. Already, many sketches have been produced but the crucial thing is to begin to make firm decisions on fabrics, textures, and colors. The direction comes from Ralph.

Three months before the designing begins in earnest, the fabric designers and Max go to Italy carrying clues to the future: antique swatches, areas of color, cashmere sweaters, anything Ralph has pinpointed as a possible direction, ready to work with the mills to produce what are known as blankets—huge pieces of cloth specially woven to show the variations in colors and textures they will have spent days discussing. When all the decisions are made and the design team has returned to New York, the mill will put all the ideas into production. When, three months on, the blankets arrive in America they are cut up into small squares for Ralph and the team to work with. It is at this point that concepts and stories are discussed. A multitude of sketches follow and key ideas for garments are experimented with in muslin. Once the sketch is perfected and the muslin is created it will be cut in the chosen cloth and shown to Ralph, who rarely sees anything at muslin stage. This is the critical moment, when the first signs show themselves of a tension that will over the next weeks build up into a tidal wave. The first fittings are the moment when everybody sees whether the hours of thought, discussion and elimination have been leading in the right direction. And, as Gerri admits, "It's a complex process because everything is developing all the time and what Ralph saw and liked two weeks earlier might no longer seem relevant now."

"I love that jacket" can quickly become "I guess it should be longer" and, even, "I don't think it's working." Because he is known for his perfectly cut jackets, they are most important for Ralph. He and his Italian tailor, who has been with him for over twenty-five years and, in the opinion of many in the design team, understands Ralph better than anyone, give infinite time to what might seem an esoteric perfectionism: the cut of a lapel… the way a button sits. For both men, there are no shortcuts. Every detail has to be perfect. Changes occur. Modifications are made. Each and every change is drawn and the revision pinned up on the wall—which is the area to which Ralph gravitates not only when he arrives at the session but at every break in the proceedings. At every point everything is presented to Ralph. The words "This is what we're thinking" become as insistent as a Greek chorus. The mood of the new collection gradually emerges, helped by the sketches which are so essential in fleshing out everyone's thinking. Fluid, elegant, and full of movement, they bring the line to life. They also focus the whole team—general ideas, broad-ranging conversations all disappear as everyone becomes increasingly aware that things are coming together; although, as one of the team says, "You never feel it is all together." The moment has come for specifics, where sketches and fabrics are married, along with buttons and all other details of the garment. Production now has a place from which to start. The "specs" continue as the ideas evolve and the details are firmed up: On the technical sketches, the size of the collar, the shape of the lapel, the number of buttons, and the length of the zipper are all recorded. Every time Ralph approves a sketch another "spec" is added to the collection.

The fittings are the most nerve-racking of all the stages in creating a collection, at Ralph Lauren just as with other designers. This is when the finished—or even half-finished—garments come from the workroom, where, with over 70 percent of the workforce being Italian-speaking, the levels of workmanship and the degree of volatility are equally high, to be tried on by the house model for Ralph's critical reaction. It can be a good time, or not. Quite often, out of ten garments, he might respond to as few as three. This always sends a mild panic through the team ranks as

116

Above: Making the collection: the Ralph Lauren workrooms.

everyone knows that time is slipping by and that for a collection of between 65 and 75 outfits, many of which will include skirts and jackets, about 140 patterns have to be produced, ready to be made up into fabric. They also know that if Ralph is interested in even as many as 200 ideas, all of them will be made into samples. Ex-staff from the past recall collections when more than 30 samples, often made up in expensive cashmere, could be dismissed because Ralph did not think they were right. They were not recut or adapted. Although perfectly made, if they didn't please, they were dumped. Ralph Lauren's business was always a luxury one at every level. Even today, Gerri Anderson says, "We could find ourselves making a thousand samples because if Ralph likes a jacket and its pattern he'll want to see it in two or three fabrics. Each fabric means another pattern, another sample. They are what we call multiples. The original pattern could give rise to another two hundred—and so on."

After the show there are further adjustments. Buffy, the Polo merchandiser, and the design team sit down, look at the line that went down the runway and decide where there are gaps that need to be filled. "Do we need more skirts on the line…? We have to have more pants…. What do we need to round out this line and make it merchandisable?"

No one is working in the dark, of course. Merchandising projections are largely given before the show. There is a main buying office for all the Polo stores in the United States, which is generally just called "the store" and which buys for every shop in the country, from New York to Hawaii. London and Paris have their own buyers, who join with key retailers like Bloomingdale's and Saks for their buying days. As Gerri says, "Nobody pre-buys Collection. Even the store won't really have a clue what's in the Collection until it actually goes down the runway." Before that happens there is one final, vital canter to the starting post. Intense, emotional, the final fittings— which include making choices on accessories; models, their make-up, and hair; which garments will actually appear on the runway and in what order; how they will be grouped; what music will be played—are a form of pure theater, of the absurd and of cruelty.

It is an ordeal for everyone. Enthusiasms wane, spirits slump, and tempers flare. Emotions run high even though they are normally controlled. Anxieties are rampant. The reason is that everyone, starting with Ralph, knows that they have a finite amount of time to get everything right. Experience has taught them that nothing will run smoothly to plan. There will be hitches and disappointments. Outworkers in New Jersey will run behind time; samples will not be properly made; models who looked great last season won't look right this. But if there are problems, there are also joys. Handbags are delivered. As they are taken out of their protective felt covers there is a communal sigh: their perfection is beyond anything even the designer envisaged. A new model appears who captures Ralph's imagination. Everyone is elated; they have had the spirit of the collection clarified—the thing that everyone prays for because they know it gives a focus to all they do. Above all, there is that late moment after a long day when Ralph winds everything up with a weary half-smile and a simple "Okay" and, emotionally, regardless of the day's tussles, everybody in the room is brother or sister in one close-knit, emotionally dependent family.

New York Fashion Week stretches for well over a week as an increasing number of designers are added to the schedule in order to take advantage of the influx of international press and store buyers who arrive every season. Ralph Lauren always shows in the middle of the week, on

"He comes in, listens to what the design team say, spends a great deal of time examining the boards and then begins to pull out ideas."

Wednesday, at 10.00 a.m. As befits such an important figure, it is a prestigious spot, holding the week together. Its timing is also important. The Ralph Lauren show is the first of the day. This means that newspapers the world over have no difficulty in ensuring that it is featured in their first editions. The period between the previous Sunday and the final checks that take place in the small hours of the night before the show is for everyone involved a treadmill of endless decision-making, as everything is queried in a group determination to remove all weaknesses and flaws, pre-empt possible criticism, and obviate any risk of anything slipping through unchecked. Fashion shows are exercises in perfection, and everything must be done to prevent even the slightest imperfection destroying the dream.

In order for all of this to be achieved, the three days before the presentation are reminiscent of a film set, with extras and technicians on hand, waiting to be called. Or perhaps they are more like a film itself, with Ralph as male lead, Buffy as chief co-star, and the models as the female leads. And, like making a film, there are bursts of febrile activity, followed by periods of calm and long periods of waiting, in limbo, while others are working fiendishly in other spots. If it were a movie, it would have to be called *Decisions*. That is precisely what the three-day lead-up to the show is about. The location is 550 Seventh Avenue, which is where the workrooms and fitting rooms are. It is very different from 650 Madison Avenue in both atmosphere and personnel.

This is the coalface—or as near to it as high fashion gets—where the drama is subdued but no less intense for that; where chit-chat gives way to serious thought expressed in terse and direct language; where tensions are briefly relieved by laughter; where, as the days of graft grind on, a feeling of shared joys and disappointments shows itself in great warmth and closeness—much of it emanating from Ralph Lauren himself. He, above all, knows how hard his staff are working to help interpret and realize what he wishes to create and he takes every opportunity to reduce the stress and keep morale high. He is, as the fifties' Spanish designer Balenciaga famously said of himself, the general to his loyal army.

Watching the process evolve over the three days preceding the show is a cineaste's experience, alternatively emotional, creative, intense, and slack, as the rhythm of the days quickens and slows, seems to stand still, and then regenerates itself with fiendish animation. In brief, what happens during these long and intensive days is that everything that will appear in the show comes in front of the informal panel of experts that will help Ralph decide how the show will be formed and in what order the different groups of clothes will be marshaled and sent down the runway on the Wednesday morning. The personnel involved changes as people leave to chase up specific items, explain to the workroom what is in Ralph's mind, and endlessly telephone suppliers, outworkers, model agencies, and a host of other ancillary helpers, many of whom never appear in person. Buffy, Ralph, and Max are always present; so, normally, are the sketchers Audrey and Alistair as well as Julia Montgomery who has been with Ralph for twelve years, and Alta Hagan who assists design development and has been with him for six. It is their job to help create a runway choice which will edit a 100 strong personality looks down to the 65 or 70 which will actually appear.

It is remarkable how consistent the choice tends to be. For weeks, Ralph has entered this small mirrored room with tables along the walls and a row of chairs reminiscent of those in a doctor's waiting room. His first action is to look at the drawings pinned on the walls, an embryonic collection regularly and ruthlessly reviewed. As he walks along praising and rejecting,

Max uses yellow Post-it tabs to record his decisions. Like a game of snakes and ladders, they appear on certain drawings—a heart drawn in felt tip for the ones which enthuse Ralph, a question mark for those for which he expresses reservations, and a cross for those which seem too doubtful to go any further. These things change over the days and even in the final countdown, by which time drawings have been replaced by polaroids, considerable juggling and realigning takes place.

By this stage everything is seen on the two house models. They put on the clothes, they walk, they stand, they answer Ralph's questions about how the garment feels and whether or not they enjoy wearing it. The last raises their role into something rather important. Young, fashionably aware, they give answers that supply him with vital information. No showing takes place without questions: "How do you like it? Do those shoes feel better with it?" Somebody says, "It looks cute." Two different shoe styles are held up. "Which do you like?" She points. "This one." "It's sparkly, like a court jester," one of the group adds. A row of pearls is held up by Buffy. She says nothing as she looks at Ralph, waiting for his reaction. After a pause, he says, "I like it." "Do we want pearls at the ears?" she asks. The model stands stock still, gazing at her reflection in the full-length mirror. Ralph moves toward her and pulls her hair back from her face and neck. "That's great. I love it," he says as Buffy gives the model the earrings. Ralph smiles. "Fabulous," he says quietly.

The next garment is black. Even as the model is walking into the room, Ralph reacts. "That collar needs to be white. Double organza. It must be white," half-turning to Max who agrees: "I know it." "This is dynamite," somebody says. Ralph smiles at the group. There are now eighteen people in the room, all concentrating on one model. "It's very marine. Very Riviera." Ralph reacts immediately. "It's not too Chanel, is it?" he asks sharply. He walks over to the polaroids of the entire collection, checking the mood of the clothes. Others in the group are bent over the shoes lined up beneath the accessories table. "We're going to be in shoe heaven this season!" A dreamy voice, "I'm shopping already. I can't get enough of these shoes."

Ralph is playing with the polaroids as if he were playing solitaire. He has fanned them out across a table and is making families, stories with them, watched intently by Max. Always the stories are questioned as he asks, "Is it too twenties and thirties? Too Chanel?" "It's not Chanel," Buffy says firmly. "It's more Coco. It's more herself and her personal style. How she and her friends dressed. Their lifestyle." He picks up a polaroid. "Do we have anything else with a bow?" "We have to talk about it," Max says. He points to a polaroid. "There's this dress coming in." "You guys like it?" Ralph asks, passing it around. The model has appeared in a new dress. Ralph moves restlessly toward her. "What do you think of this?" "I like it," she replies. "Why?" he responds immediately. All critical attention is focused on the dress. "It looks dowdy." "Old." "Aren't we getting a bit Prada-ish here?" He listens to the comments, sighs, and says, "It doesn't excite me. It's pretty but it's ordinary." Buffy says, "It would look more Ralph Lauren with pinstripes." As the model leaves the room, Max says quietly, "I know what's wrong. It's a little light. It needs an edgier girl if it is to work."

Ralph is back at the polaroids, the working tool. While they wait for the model to get dressed, he talks to his two lieutenants, Buffy and Max. Repositioning a polaroid he says, "It's better in this category. It makes it very strong. Very chic." He becomes excited. "Look how these work together.

Right: Ralph Lauren Collection, fall 2001.

This is an amazing story. This is so new. This tells you the whole show. Right here. It's all here. This is the show, Max." Euphoria flows, the faces of the trusted ones loosen up and relax.

Twenty minutes later, the handbag samples arrive. As they are unwrapped, each is greeted with cries of enthusiasm. Ralph holds them up against Buffy and examines them in the mirror. "Do we have any black in this one? How do we transition from brown to black?" "That doesn't bother me," Max says. Ralph is unsure. "But everybody loves this, Ralph, it's so chic." "Okay. Maybe it's good. But it isn't going anywhere. Not yet." He holds up another sample. "This is important. It's a happening thing. We've gotta be more graphic here, to get the message through." The concentration is broken by the appearance of a model in a suit, caught in at the back with large paperclips. She has been brought in by the model agency for an audition. There is total silence. Ralph looks intently at her face. New and inexperienced, she blushes. He takes pity. "Can I see you walk?" he asks quietly. She walks up and down the room. "Thank you," he says, and smiles. It is only when she is totally out of earshot that he almost whispers to Max, "She's a little blank. Too delicate." "No," agrees Max, rejecting her not because she isn't good, but because she is not right for releasing the mood of the clothes on the runway.

The house model comes in, wearing a white pant suit. She immediately has Ralph's total concentration. Nothing is said for at least 30 seconds. Everyone in the room seems frozen, waiting for his word to loosen them up. Eventually, he speaks. "Maybe I want a skirt." He shows a polaroid to Buffy. "Put this skirt with it." She finds it and holds it up against the model. "That's cool," Ralph says. "That's great. Okay. Let's try it." As he is about to dismiss the model, Buffy says, "Do you have a problem with the cuff?" "It bothered me to begin with," he admits. "But now I like it." He pauses and adds, with some animation, "You know what I don't like? You can't push it up." "We could make an opening. We could loosen it," Max says. Ralph changes his mind. "No, leave it like that. It's good. It's distinctive that way." Just as the model is turning to go, he turns to Buffy. "Can you bring me the white shoes? I want to see the white shoes."

They change his perception. He is clearly uncertain now. He asks the model, "Do you like it?" "I like it a lot." He points to the belt. "You know," he says to the room in general, "this is bothering me." Buffy holds up various belts. "I think the white is most exciting," he says. Buffy is not happy. "Don't you think it kinda disappears in white? The black is stronger." Sensing Ralph's uncertainty, everyone seems ready with a comment. "Make it shorter." "Is it going to have a collar tomorrow?" "Maybe it doesn't need a collar." "And maybe it does. That's why we're doing it." "Is there going to be a brown version?" It's an ongoing chorus—half Greek theater half *Pajama Game*. Ralph moves back to the polaroids. "My only question—it's not even a question, really," he intones, "is: the white looks so good, dynamic, so chic—do we want more white?" "We could maybe do with some more white," a troubled voice offers. Ralph replies, "My concern here is repetition." Buffy nods. "Maybe it could go up here," she points to the second of the four rows of polaroids. Ralph shuffles the polaroids like a Reno cardshark. "I think we should do it," he says in a decisive voice. "But it doesn't go here. So here's the issue," he points at the polaroids. "Do you like it here—or here?" The minute decision-making stretches through the afternoon into the evening. At intervals, people retreat to eat something from a constantly replenished salad bar in the main entrance. Ralph is brought food and water. He barely touches either. At one point, he is given an iced cappuccino. Only 30 seconds later does it register. "Who gave me this? I don't even know." He smiles. "They could be handing me poison!"

Previous pages: Ralph Lauren Collection, spring 2001.

124

By Tuesday, the final fittings are done. The Italian workforce has produced miracles. All the clothes will be ready on time. To achieve it, many of the tailors have worked all night. Everything is calm. There is no sense of panic. Models arrive throughout the day. Ralph receives them courteously. "Hi," is his standard greeting. He makes a decision quickly. They have to walk up and down the crowded room only once. Only when they have gone does he talk to the model consultant: "She's nice. Very sleek. Classy-looking." "What I really need is short hair. That's the look." "We've got about six girls with short hair." He frowns: "I didn't like her hair." "Color or length?" "Both." "It was done in LA…." "I really liked that earlier one. The one who wore the striped dress. She looked gorgeous." "She's lost a lot of weight but she does still have a bust."

By this stage, there are certain keywords which crop up repeatedly: Park Avenue… sophisticated… Riviera… They are the mood of the show, something which it is vital the music reflects. Both Ralph's sons get involved, very aware of how crucial it is to get it right. "Dad shows us the clothes, then gives us the keywords," Andrew says. "The music must never be too literal. He wants a hip, current mix with a Sinatra-style sophistication. Suppose it's Mexican, we have to turn it on its head, add some hip-hop. A club mix. An underbeat. He hates being old-fashioned."

As the final, irreversible decisions are made about what will appear on the runway, the observations, half in code, move at increasing speed:

"I could take the shirt and put it with the pants?"

"Now you love it."

"We have a dilemma: where to show it?"

"It would have more power here."

"It would look really cool there, with all the lace."

"It doesn't go with that group."

"If you gave me a white leather skirt…."

"I disagree."

"We're showing a white leather trench, here. Right?"

"What are we doing this for?"

"You sure are pushing that look, girl."

"I'm going for it. Tell Ralph, so I'm not alone."

Editing a collection is like reducing a sauce. You know you have caught the essence when all the flavors keep their distinction but blend with the others. By this point, Ralph is feeling buoyant, even jokey. When the house model announces she has to leave because she is booked to do a show, he says to her: "How can you do this to me? What am I to do? Do you have any sisters?" "No, I have a brother. He's six foot four." Ralph grins. "He'll do. Send him along. What's in the water over there?"—the girl is Scandinavian—"How do you get so tall?" "It's more what we eat." "What?" She pauses… "Potatoes." "You're supposed to get that way with potatoes? Now she tells me!"

While everybody is waiting for the new model to be dressed, Ralph begins to ham things up, as if giving an interview. "What's my inspiration this season?" he asks, in the voice of Robin Williams in *Dead Poets' Society*. "Fear. Fear of going out of business. That's my inspiration." He laughs. "Do you really want to know? Do you seriously wanna know?" He sounds like Sinatra. "Give me another mike here. Fear… fear of herringbone…." He becomes serious as the new model appears, as dark as the previous one was blonde. He spins round. "Wow! That's gorgeous," he says, as she swings her hips to make the skirt move. "How would you walk in this?" he asks. "She's Brazilian,

Left: Ralph Lauren Collection, fall 2001.

Previous page: Ralph Lauren Collection, fall 2001.

Ralph. She doesn't speak English." "What language?" "Portuguese." He takes two strides toward the mirror, throwing wide his arms theatrically. "Portuguese! The only language I don't know. Russian? I could have done it…." He ties a scarf around the model's neck. "I think it's beautiful." He looks at Buffy and says with mock hostility, "You got a problem?" Then, in an exaggerated South American accent, "I like eet. I think very chic." Buffy replies quickly, "I guess that's the Portuguese version, yeah?" The model swings her hips again, to regain their attention. "I feel," she says, "I want her to wear this in the show." Ralph decides, "Just avoid it looking like the Mexican hat dance." "We have too many beaded, Ralph," somebody says. "This collection is going to be big," he replies. "I want to be able to sell it, Ralph." "You'll sell it. Just twist their arms. If they don't, you don't get paid. That's all." Then, serious again, he asks the model to raise her skirt. "Lift it higher. Higher." There is a general murmur of approval. Every change and adjustment is photographed and the new polaroid pinned to the old one as a record of the change.

It's almost the end of the day. Things wind down, final dresses are checked. Ralph makes ready to go. At the door he turns, half waves and as a thank you says, "I hate leaving, but I'm happy to go. The best three days I've had in… at least three days." In a corner of the room, Max is checking the carbon-fiber handbags. "How superb is this?" he asks the room in general, as he holds one up. "Such a message. Such a message."

The morning of the Ralph Lauren Collection show begins early at the venue, 387 West Broadway. For many of the background players there has been no night, as they worked from dusk to dawn on lights, construction, and a myriad of minor details. Electricians and carpenters have swarmed over the area, positioning pieces of equipment, checking, repositioning, all fueled by endless coffee, bagels, or French fries. There have been tensions, clashes of personality, disagreements, swearing—and a lot of good humor of the "It's a shit job but somebody has to do it" kind. For most of the night, people have worked with a stoical determination, always watching the clock, always aware that in this job there can be no compromises or shortcuts. It is not just a question of safety, although City of New York by-laws are tough—in a few hours there will be an audience of several hundred in this space—what drives everybody forward on an energy high is the knowledge that there can be no more delays, no postponements. The show must go on and, whereas many designers run very late—often for reasons over which they have no control—the Ralph Lauren tradition is that the show goes out on time.

Shortly after 6.00 a.m. members of the Lauren staff begin to arrive. They are the first of the stormtroopers. The majority will appear between 7.00 a.m. and 8.00 a.m. Greetings are relaxed and jokey, there is lots of chat and gossip, but that does not hide the fact that everybody in the room is totally focused. There are no second chances. What is not right will remain forever wrong. There are no second takes, no reruns. Each and every person in the room is determined that, if by some mischance anything goes wrong, the fault will not be his or hers. As if to emphasize the seriousness of the event, all the Ralph Lauren staff are in black—color of authority and efficiency—with white tags around their necks, pinned to their sweaters or swinging at their hips—fashion people style themselves in all particulars and at all times of day. Serious as the final preparations are, there is nothing somber or even nervous in the atmosphere. The huge white loft where the girls are made up and have their hair done contains about a hundred people, including

Fashion shows are exercises in perfection, and everything must be done to avoid even the slightest imperfection destroying the dream.

key players such as Buffy, huge mug of coffee in her hand, wearing headset and mike so that communication is instant. The atmosphere has a party feel to it. There is chat … gossip … jokes … gossip … anxious consultations over hair … gossip—about parties, other shows, discos, clothes, and above all, boyfriends—"He was so cute and chunky"—all the trivial things hairdressers and models find with which to twitter away the time and prevent themselves thinking too seriously.

Hair and make-up are the first steps toward preparation for the catwalk because they take the most time. The middle of the room is dominated by long trestle tables with rows of high stools for the models to sit on so that their heads can be seen in the long low mirrors. Models arrive with their agents or minders, and are ticked off the list, before being sent to hair and make-up for the transformation to begin. It is a fascinating process. Girls who arrived looking totally unmemorable apart from their height, often with the sort of faces which would go unremarked on the subway, gauche and even diffident, are slowly transformed into beautiful narcissistic creatures, preening before the mirror, bathing in the enthusiastic comments of hairdressers. As the transformation continues, there is an almost palpable sense of collective rising self-esteem.

While this is going on, more donuts, bagels, coffee, and cigarettes are consumed. There is a great deal of animated chat. Agents and backstage cameramen are filming, taking polaroids, and generally hyping up the atmosphere merely by their presence. The initial cry, "All right, you guys! Rehearsal. All the girls downstairs," receives a sluggish response. Everyone is having too much fun. The atmosphere is party—helped by champagne for those who can face it so early in the day (a surprising number of people). But this is serious work and, after a little chivvying and a few more shouted instructions, most of the girls who have already been made-up troop down the narrow steps to the backstage area, where all the racks containing the clothes are waiting, attended by the dressers whose responsibility it is to ensure that each girl is in her correct outfit, with the right shoes and accessories, ready for her exit onto the catwalk. Everything is in a clear plastic bag. Twenty staff have been on site since 3.00 a.m., checking and rechecking that each bag was complete. There is a long line of beautiful girls waiting to use the loo. A tough voice cries, "You guys! Go to the bathroom after rehearsal, OK? Chop, chop!" and what has to be the most glamorous line in all of New York at that moment breaks up. "All right, you guys," the voice continues, "Start line-up." As the models are being marshaled the dressers are being given their final brief: "… I'm assuming you've checked everything, including the shoes. If you have any questions, ask. Take the tags off everything." Each dress on its hanger has a polaroid taken of it in the final fitting so that the dressers have a visual record of exactly how the model must look. "Check the shoes in the picture," the instructions continue, "Make sure you have what's in the picture. If not, talk to me. Remember, we don't have all the shoes, so the girls will drop them here, as they come off."

There is a blast of music, which promptly stops. The dressers scurry back to their stands and start checking the contents of their plastic accessories bags against the polaroid of each outfit, making sure that they have everything. The atmosphere is changing. There is a growing feeling of purpose and anticipation. Ralph, who has been here for some time, walks around, quietly and with apparent confidence, chatting to individuals in a low voice, dealing with queries, giving the quick soundbite to the broadcasters and being most reminiscent of Shakespeare's *Henry V* as he walked the lines of his soldiers on the night before the Battle of Agincourt. It becomes apparent that what he has, possibly much more so than other designers, is the quiet confidence of the born leader. People trust him. They rely on him. They follow him. And he inspires them. That there is none of the frantic panic, hysteria, and bad temper that normally characterize behind-the-scenes pre-show jitters is entirely due to Ralph Lauren's leadership skills. He sets the tone and creates the carapace that everyone gladly assumes. Quietly, without any brouhaha, he becomes the chief of this disparate and often mismatched clan and he sets a tone of purposeful focus. Above all, he instills dignity and calm.

The music starts again. Ralph moves to the front of house and joins Max Wilson and Andrew—who has been largely responsible for creating the music for his father—ready for the models, who are being organized and put in line by Buffy, to come out. At the end of the runway the press photographers are arriving, marshaled by men in T-shirts with "Crew" or "Team" across their chests. They are the sort of men to whom even the most obstreperous photographer listens. The lights flick on and off as electricians on worryingly high ladders make final adjustments to the lighting. The models bob out in a line. They are all wearing the Pink Pony T-shirt which launched a new campaign against cancer which Ralph Lauren has created. Otherwise, they are in jeans and sneakers. All have had their faces done, some still have their hair in rollers but already the transformation from rather dumb duck to *soignée* swan is well underway.

The "walk through" is precisely that. There is no stopping. Its purpose is twofold: for Ralph to see the girls and make any decisions—or last-minute adjustments—as to who should come out with whom, and for the girls, not all of whom have worked for him before, to familiarize themselves with the catwalk. In their semi-transformed state they look movingly vulnerable, with their delicate small heads and torsos, and legs just too long, like Bambis tripping across a clearing in the woods.

Behind the scenes, more people have arrived. All are elegantly dressed, many of the men in suits. Because this collection is almost entirely in black and white, Ralph himself is dressed in that way. Looking as elegant as a Deauville yachtsman—casual but debonair—he wears a white top and black pants, a subtle reversal of the way they used to be worn in the twenties. He remains outwardly calm as he smiles and greets well-wishers with a few relaxed words. He talks a lot to Andrew but is ready to give his full attention when Buffy or other key members of his staff come up to him to discuss a point or receive clarification.

The models are now hovering around their racks of clothes, each of which has their name— Rhea… Raica… Trish… Malgosia…—scrawled on a card along with the name of the dressers— Anna… Valentina. The language is polyglot. Snatches of Spanish, Italian, and Portuguese float in and out of the predominant English—a reflection not only of the fact that the modeling profession is totally multinational but also an indication of how many models now come from South America. Most of the 32 girls have two changes, although one or two, whom Ralph sees as especially right for this collection, have three or even more. Girls and dressers check all details while things are still calm. When they are being dressed during the show, a process that usually takes just over two minutes, there is no time to start looking for lost items. The details are all clearly written out: the number of the outfit, the color, the fabric, and, finally, the name of the item, such as the Hayley pant. Shoe sizes and whether or not ears are pierced are all recorded.

Left: Gwyneth Paltrow after winning an Oscar for *Shakespeare In Love* in 1999.

The plastic bags contain shoes and jewelry but, as Ralph has decided to use real pearls with some of the clothes, the models are instructed, "Get pearls at the door if not in bags." They are on a table just in front of the exit where the girls step out onto the catwalk—and they are guarded.

The general chat and joking have gone. Conversations are short and precise. A hairdresser asks, "Who do you want me to do next?" Someone in make-up asks, "Where's Rhea?" An agent argues, "Look, I do not want to make her nervous at this point…." In a subconscious gesture, hairdressers take combs out of the back pocket of their jeans, along with a waterspray bottle, and almost absent-mindedly comb and recomb hair already perfect to the non-expert eye. Some models are being interviewed for television, their high-pitched baby voices transforming them from goddesses to Barbie dolls. Someone says to Ralph, "We're all ready to go but two of the models just got here so we're waiting for them." Much of the talk now is to keep the energy level high. Agents and hairdressers are hyping the models up, getting the adrenalin going. Someone says, "You look pretty relaxed, Ralph." He grins and replies, "I'm not. I'm not." Buffy circles the room like a sheepdog, always ending at Ralph, reporting, commenting.

Ricky arrives, in the same negative-positive outfit as Ralph, wearing a white shirt and black skirt. With her are David, formal in a navy pinstripe suit, and Dylan. The photographers home in on the family. The show is slated to start at 10.00 a.m. By 10.10, the dressers have begun. Snatches of conversation rise in the air out of the general conversational hubbub: "Where is?.. I saw … Forget it …." The board containing the polaroids of the 63 outfits to be shown is being checked by Buffy, who is making a note of the really fast changes. Yfka, the model Ralph considers best personifies his look this season, starts the show and has five changes. Ralph gestures to a model, "I want to see her hair." Girl and hairdresser stand before him anxiously. He leans forward and pushes the model's hair up at the sides, lets it drop—and immediately has a more natural look. He smiles sympathetically at the hairdresser. By 10.20 the girls who will go out in the first group are dressed. "OK! Ready to start. Let's have the line-up!" The models are told, "You guys walk up here." Ralph and Max are at the exit with Buffy, a closed-circuit TV next to them. Buffy calls out the models' names, like a schoolmistress checking off the list of her pupils on an impossibly exotic school trip. As Yfka takes her chewing gum out of her mouth, Ralph smoothes her hair. Like every other girl, she passes a quality control line-up beginning with Buffy, followed by Max, and finalized by Ralph. Buffy has lint-chasers and clothes brushes in her hands, a stylist carries a jar of pommade for smoothing down hair and a clutch of pins, Ralph submits the model to his final razor-sharp gaze. "OK guys! We're starting!" For the first time, he shows nervousness and emotion as he watches on the monitor as the girls go down the runway.

The speed, energy, and concentration of the next twenty minutes is overwhelming. Girls step elegantly off the runway and break into a gallop as their dressers wait for them. There is much pushing and tugging. Clothes are whipped off backs while new ones are waiting to be thrown over heads. Shoes are forced open to make them fit. Pearls are madly swapped. As he's checking her hair, Ralph quietly asks Yfka, "How are they reacting? OK?" Suddenly, all the girls are lined up for the finale. They step out to enthusiastic applause which quickly turns into a standing ovation. Smiling, but with tears in his eyes, Ralph Lauren walks out onto the runway, dazzled for a second by the lights, and raises his hand, waving in acknowledgment of the support.

selling the dream

The last twenty years of the twentieth century will probably be seen as Ralph Lauren's greatest decades, the time when he earned the comment that he was the man "who giftwrapped taste and sold it to the Americans." Clever as that remark is, it tells merely a part of the success story of Ralph Lauren at that time. They were the years when he branched out into Europe and the Far East, as well as developing his business in America. They were the years when his retailing skills almost overshadowed the clothes; years in which his approach to merchandising affected the entire fashion industry, as his ideas were filched and used by retailers across the globe.

The event of the decade for Ralph Lauren in both personal and business terms was the opening in 1986 of his flagship store, the former Rhinelander mansion, at 867 Madison Avenue—a venture so breathtakingly bold and so splendidly achieved that it dwarfed everything else. It was a piece of folly which was turned to triumphant success by a singlemindedness almost amounting to tunnel vision on Lauren's part. It put the indelible seal of success on him as one of the world's most inspired retailers. If the Lauren empire had collapsed at that point, leaving only the Rhinelander, the building would have ensured his name for history.

It was a name that had grown phenomenally in the first years of the eighties as a form of Lauren-mania swept the media. Maybe because his private life was kept so resolutely private—apart from the rare, carefully coordinated picture stories of him and his family in their newest home, which were given only to the most reliable of the top magazines—interviews with him still remained exclusive but became slightly easier to secure.

"This company is nothing more than this life and style. The formula he developed gave the consumers confidence."

It must be remembered that the eighties were the time when the media suddenly discovered fashion designers as the new source of envy and adulation for their readers or viewers, taking the place of film stars, pop singers and even sportsmen—none of whom could bring the frisson of power that designers now wielded over, it would seem, the entire civilized world. The very noun designer achieved even greater power as an adjective prefixing virtually any object: designer colors, designer bathrooms and designer envelopes were what everybody wanted, as the designer label took hold of the imagination of consumers everywhere. Although all designers were hyped there was no label that had the payback of Polo—the symbol of the class and assurance the longing for which underpinned the whole edifice of logo hysteria. No label had such resonance. In fact, Polo defined what designer labels were about—and every other designer and manufacturer in the world—from Chanel and Gucci, to Klein and Vuitton—knew that it was the benchmark to which they had somehow to climb. It was effortlessly pre-eminent.

It may have appeared that Polo had reached talismanic status with ease and speed but, of course, it wasn't as simple as it seemed. If Ralph Lauren appeared to his rival designers to have vaulted the hurdles with effortless grace, the fact was that his first mention, in the menswear newspaper *Daily News Record*, had been in 1964. When he opened the doors of the Rhinelander mansion as his glittering dream made concrete, Ralph Lauren had been working in the business for a dozen years. He had earned his celebrity. He had proved his multifaceted abilities. He had not only created a multi-billion dollar business, he had made his attitudes synonymous with the upwardly mobile dreams of millions of people. Even members of ethnic minorities, far outside the charmed WASP circle that Lauren had glamorized, felt there could be a place for them in his enchanted world. But perhaps the most warming achievement for Ralph Lauren personally was that, David-like, he had taken on the Goliath of the fashion world and had won. Despite all the experienced wise counsel that had assured him he could not, he now had the answer to the question once posed to him: how far can you get with prices pitched at your level? He didn't need words in order to reply. His achievements made the incontrovertible riposte: to the very top.

Lance Isham believes that Lauren's success springs from a single mindedness both inadvertent and unavoidable, being at the very root of the man's personality. As he sees it, "This company is nothing more than his life and his style. The formula he developed gave the consumers confidence. It showed them how to approach fashion and style, because everything he offered them had the sense of longevity, simplicity, quality and confidence, whether it was in home, apparel or accessories." It also had the discreet charm of the man, softly endorsing every new addition to his range, every change of direction. He became the undisputed Pied Piper of Hamelin for the middle classes and those aspiring to join them, piping a seductive tune which led them up his pre-selected paths, leading them toward things they only half knew they desired and rarely actually required. This was his great skill: to present people with choices they had never previously considered and to make them so desirable that they could no longer live happily without them. The addiction was so instant and so complete, if it weren't offensive to this most inoffensive of world-class figures, Ralph Lauren could be called the visual crack dealer to a whole generation. By the time a journalist writing in *The New Republic* in 1988 had coined the expression "the Laurenification of America," it was already out of date—his influence had spread much further than his own shores.

The first major drive to take Ralph Lauren beyond America was focussed on London. Ralph had decided in the late seventies that, although as a sales field Europe would probably never be as strong as America, for prestige a foothold there would be extremely useful. He knew he needed a serious retail presence in Europe and, being a strong Anglophile, thought that he should open in a store in London. He began negotiations with Browns of South Molton Street, owned by Joan and Sidney Burstein.

Joan Burstein, the doyenne of London fashion retailing, has an eye for fashion which is unrivaled. Even in the late seventies, she had, by her shrewd choice of international designers whom she promoted exclusively in her shop, set London on its path as one of the world's top fashion retailing cities. She was known for her eye, her refined charm and her unflinching business sense, as she still is today, twenty years after her first meeting with Ralph Lauren.

Sarah Harrison, who worked in PR for Mrs Burstein in the late seventies and early eighties before moving to Ralph Lauren, recalls, "Mrs B was very impressed by New York designers at that point. We stocked Norma Kamali, Zoran and Perry Ellis and they all did well. She was very keen to add Calvin Klein and Ralph, especially as Ann Boyd, the influential journalist, gave them huge coverage in the English press week after week. Naturally, Browns was attractive to Ralph because, frankly, they were the only people doing interesting things in retail in London, with the exception of Joseph, who had a very different approach." Browns became even more attractive when they introduced Calvin Klein's range in 1980. The two men were rivals, not on a personal but on a business level, and Ralph felt that if his rival were in London, then he should also be there. Joan Burstein agreed. He was the last arrow she needed to fill her quiver of American talent.

Robert Forrest, who worked closely with Joan Burstein as her fashion buyer, recalls that when they first started to visit New York for the fashion shows they knew more about Calvin than Ralph Lauren and, in fact, used to go to Studio 54 with Klein whenever they were in town. "It wasn't until we started going to New York that we realized how very important Ralph was as an American designer," he says. "We were very impressed, not just because he was so successful but because he was so professional. I remember we went to see his Santa Fe collection at the Pierre hotel. We loved it, because all those knits and chambrays were not something we'd seen in Europe. They were very individual and, to our eyes, very American. We went backstage after the show and it was agreed we should meet Ralph and Peter Strom at that time at Ralph Lauren, to discuss possibilities. Ralph said how much he'd love to have a shop in England and Mrs B said, 'And we would love to do something with you.' She was impressed by his business set-up as well as by the image and the look."

Joan Burstein remembers her first meeting with Ralph perfectly. She was amazed at his modesty. She returned to London and set about finding premises, because Ralph told her he wanted a free-standing store rather than to be part of the Browns emporium, where Calvin Klein was. She discovered that the old chemist shop, Savory and Moore, at 143 New Bond Street, set up in 1803 to minister to the needs of the royal family and aristocracy, was being forced to close down because the rent had risen too high. Joan and Sidney Burstein went to look at it and knew immediately that it had the right character for Ralph's unique fashion approach. Ralph Lauren and the Bursteins were joint partners in the venture.

Ann Boyd maintains that Ralph loved the old-world quality of the Bond Street shop with its open fires, easy chairs and copies of the daily papers. "For years it was his favorite," she claims, although it did not find favor with the English immediately. "Many of our customers found the

Just as people go to art galleries knowing that they cannot afford to buy what is on the walls, so many go to a Ralph Lauren shop in the same spirit.

prices far too high," Joan Burstein recollects. "The overheads were too great; we were all losing money. I knew it was only a question of time before we turned it around. I had total faith in him. But my husband said we couldn't hang on any longer." She loved the shop and was determined that they would give Ralph the opportunity to buy it. "I really defied my husband on this. He had a buyer but I insisted that it should be Ralph's. He found a partner, and they bought it, lock, stock and barrel in 1983. I knew he'd do well. I had much more confidence in Ralph than in Calvin, actually. He kept renewing himself whereas, with Calvin, people became bored because it was all the same."

Ralph took Sarah Harrison with him to deal with PR and persuade the English press to feature his merchandise. She recalls the problems. "In the eighties, there were considerable differences between American and British approaches to advertising and editorial," she explains. "The English press were totally independent. English journalists had no intention of being told, 'You can't put a Ralph Lauren pair of trousers with a Vivienne Westwood shirt.' The stylists on the top magazines were too powerful for that. And I think Ralph found that unsatisfactory. He always expected a terrific amount, but he has a very good spirit and a kind heart and, because he knew I was doing my best, he was always very warm." In fact, the Bond Street store survived, and has been consistently successful since the eighties.

It was in eighties' America, though, that Polo and Ralph Lauren personally became almost an institution, and a very liked one at that. Just as people go to art galleries knowing that they cannot afford to buy what is on the walls, so many go to a Ralph Lauren shop in the same spirit: to be informed and uplifted. Ralph Lauren made shopping an experience which often had nothing to do with making a purchase, just as it had been in the glory days of the great department stores of the world during the forties and fifties. What he was feeding was the universal need for aspirations. The Rhinelander store fulfilled them in every way. Its instant success proved how perfectly he understood the spirit of the age.

From the outset, the building had a romantic past, something which surely gave Ralph Lauren the first tingle of excitement, but its geographical position would normally have precluded it from any consideration as a major retail outlet. At the corner of Madison and 72nd Street, it was way above New York's shopping area. Naomi Leff, the design consultant on the project, recalls "He passed it every day on his way to work and I suppose the idea just grew gently within him. It was a major act of faith but you must never forget that with Ralph Lauren you are dealing with a man with a major vision. People said it was too big; it was in the wrong location. It was too small. He would take business away from his existing outlets; it was in the wrong location. Everybody advised against it. The decision was his alone."

Naomi Leff had worked as store designer for Bloomingdale's before leaving to form her own consultancy, so she was well aware of Ralph Lauren's approach to merchandising which, she claims, was entirely unique in the early eighties. Her first major job as an interior designer for Ralph Lauren was to create a log cabin showroom for Ralph Lauren Home, which she found exacting but extremely stimulating. "The night before the showroom was to be presented to Ralph I was working so hard I had no sleep and so, in the morning, I went home to shower and change. When I arrived, Ralph, Ricky and the kids were there and they had already moved to the second room. I walked in and there were tears in his eyes. It was very emotional for him because it wasn't just a showroom. He was seeing a new business born. So, of course, I got emotional too, especially when he said, 'how do you know about quality?' It was such a question. I remember after the presentation he said, 'Why are you sad? I sense that you are sad.' In that marvellous voice of his. I could hardly speak but I managed to say, 'Well, for me it's an end but for you it's a beginning.' To my utter amazement he replied, 'Oh, no. I have lots of work for you.'"

It was the first step in a business relationship which involved designing many of Ralph Lauren's high-class stores across the country and included both the Rhinelander and the Lodge at the family ranch in Colorado. Leff confesses that she learned a great deal from Ralph. "At that time he was unique," she claims. A key member of the team was Jeff Walker, Ralph's director of creative services, now dead, generally considered to have an infallible eye upon which Ralph relied with total trust. "They were creatively uncannily close," Ann Boyd recalls. "Not that Jeff was a 'yes' man. Just the opposite. He was one of the few who knew he had the artistic authority to tell Ralph directly what he felt—and Ralph always respected what he said." Gerry Robertson offered a retailers point of view regarding sku (stock keeping unit) capacity, merchandising and store capacity. Also on the team was Buffy who's job was to coordinate between Naomi and Jeff and most importantly Ralph.

Leff's firm was only five years old when Ralph Lauren offered her the Rhinelander. Several people, she believes, advised Ralph that she didn't have the experience for such a mammoth task but he had made his decision. If there was controversy over his choice it was nothing compared with the controversy surrounding the whole project. It was, after all, a huge gamble in every sense. In any case, Leff was simultaneously designing the Ralph Lauren store in Paris, which opened within days of the Rhinelander in the spring of 1986. Located on the corner of the rue Royale and the Place de la Madeleine, it was, if one excepts the establishment of Mainbocher in the thirties, who although born in Germany was a naturalized American, the first American designer outlet in Paris. The building, demolished and re-erected in 1913, was the original site of the Restaurant Durand, favorite haunt of turn-of-the-century politicians and intellectuals, reputedly the place where Emile Zola wrote his notorious "J'accuse" letter in the Dreyfus scandal of 1898.

The 4,000 square meter shop was set up as the European flagship store for Polo Ralph Lauren by Louis-Dreyfus Retail Inc., and was claimed by Ann Boyd, Lauren's creative director for Europe at that time, as the most sophisticated store under the designer's name, with the exception of the not yet opened Madison Avenue store. It had cost over $1 million and had all the Lauren trademarks: mahogany staircase and fittings "prefabricated in Germany," according to a report in *The Daily News Record*, "in various antique styles of the past three centuries." The report also commented, "Before the press opened, key store personnel were sent to the flea markets of Paris and London to scout for antique jewellery, perfume bottles, luggage, golf clubs, binoculars, books and other objects which are being used to enhance the presentation of the merchandise." It was the perfect curtain-raiser for what New York was to see a few days later.

The Rhinelander mansion—the only example in New York of neo-classical French architecture—was loosely modeled on the châteaux of the Loire Valley. Begun in 1895 for Mrs Gertrude Rhinelander Waldo and virtually completed in 1898, it was never lived in. Her husband having died during the years of its building, Mrs Rhinelander simply could not afford to complete it or move in. It remained entirely vacant until 1921, when some of its five storeys were let out to

Above: The exterior of the Soho store in New York.

... the devil is in the detail, and in the Rhinelander every detail had to be right.

various businesses. Before Ralph Lauren became involved with it in 1985, it had already been made both a federal and a New York landmark. At that time, the government had a tax incentive scheme for the preservation of federally landmarked buildings and, provided the work passed their tests, it paid 25 percent of the construction costs. At every stage, "before and after" pictures of all work had to be taken and submitted to the federal office in Philadelphia. The total bill was in excess of $25 million, and Ralph Lauren owned not a brick. The house had cost Mrs Rhinelander over $500,000 and was leased by the Lauren organization from its owners, a Saudi-Arabian-backed consortium called the 867 Madison Partnership, that bought the building in 1983, reputedly for a sum close to $7 million. Ralph Lauren rented it for twenty years, with a further option on the next twenty.

It was a huge gamble, not merely financially, but socially. What Ralph Lauren instructed Naomi Leff to do was virtually to create an anachronism. He wished to turn back the clock to the days at the turn of the century, when New York had many grand family homes on such a scale. Many of Ralph's friends, realizing that the only way such a building could be renovated would be to restore it to the glories of the turn-of-the-century life of high privilege, felt that he had surely made a social miscalculation. What could be accepted in a confined area of a department store would surely in an area of 20,000 square feet crush the most robust spirit and overwhelm potential customers, they argued.

They were wrong. They didn't realize what made the Lauren magic work, regardless of scale. Ralph Lauren had realized that people's romantic longing for the past had little to do with historical connections, or with the sordid facts of the story. What people wanted from the past was beauty, elegance and style. Marveling at the wealth and glamor of the past is a universal pleasure.

Ralph Lauren knew instinctively that his evocation of the upper classes in England and America from the thirties to the fifties would find an answering chord in thousands. Equally, he knew that a longing for the rural idylls of America's past could be activated in the minds and imaginations not only of Americans but of people who had never set foot in America: "I didn't succeed in business by underestimating my customers' desire for quality and excellence. People want more than you think they do." Throughout the seventies, he had presented a steady vision of how men and women might look. Now, in the eighties, he placed his clothes in their setting, rather as a producer places his characters on a stage. This great leap forward was activated by the Rhinelander. And it was done by Lauren with a true sense of responsibility. As Charles Fagan puts it, "He allows the world to walk into the most extraordinarily fitted glamorous house of the sort you could only see in books or are allowed to experience in house tours. He allows them to educate themselves in quality. And nobody has to buy. He gives them the opportunity to be exposed to quality, to grow up in quality with each visit until they become a partner. When the Rhinelander first opened a lot of people called it too exclusive and exclusionary. They couldn't have misunderstood Ralph more completely. He's a modern retailer. He's not like those old-fashioned gentlemen's stores which were almost like clubs, opening their doors only to those who they thought were worthy to be members." To take such an attitude would have been totally alien to Lauren. As Sarah Harrison recalls, "Ralph once said to me that he wanted people to be able to enjoy the same sort of life he had. It was in his gift to show people life's possibilities and he wanted to give people those possibilities, even if it was something as simple as how you could place a cushion on a chair, so that in a subtle way it enhanced your life."

As has been said so many times about Ralph Lauren, the devil is in the detail, and, in the Rhinelander every detail had to be right. Leff and her team researched the history of the building, used what scraps of internal evidence remained on which to base a reconstruction, spent days in museums and art galleries, building up dossiers of authenticity. Their brief was not just to produce for Ralph the most beautiful store in the world. He wanted it to have historic verisimilitude. All the rooms were to be kept to the residential scale of the original building. The problem was the main staircase. No trace of it remained, if, indeed, it had ever been constructed, and yet, as the main artery of the house, it had to be entirely in character. It was agreed that the best model for it was the staircase of the Connaught Hotel, where Ralph stayed whenever he visited London. Naomi Leff was dispatched to London to examine it and take photographs from which her team could produce drawings and plans to enable the workforce to reproduce it, although Buffy wound up making a poor sketch of it as the Connaught refused there quest to take photographs.

From its opening day, the Rhinelander did not merely justify Ralph's faith in his dream, it captured the imagination of New York, the United States and the fashionable world. American broadcasting networks reported it as if it were the opening of a major museum or art institution—and they were, in a way, correct to do so. The Rhinelander opening was as much an artistic event as it was a social and merchandising one. A year after its opening *Women's Wear Daily*, claiming the store to be one of Manhattan's hottest tourist attractions, said that between 1,000 and 15,000 customers went through its doors daily, shattering "expectations for its first year by doing in excess of $30 million, more than triple the pre-opening projection." The building was superb. Every detail was right. No wonder people who came to stare stayed to buy. They were buying into a cultural experience, were they not? The predominant mood was almost tranquil, as, overawed by what they saw, customers stopped talking, spoke in whispers as if in a church, or merely silently pointed.

And those who came slowly began to conceive Lauren's statement, "this store is everything I ever wanted to say in my life: a total fulfilment. It's not about clothes. It's about elegance and classicism." It is also about accessibility. As a former head of advertising for Calvin Klein told *Fortune* magazine in 1996, "Ralph's world is not unapproachable or scary. Everything is done with the promise of good taste." That, in itself, of course, flatters the potential customer who sees Ralph Lauren figuratively extending a benevolent hand and offering to draw him into the privileged enclave because—and this is the important thing—Ralph thinks he is worthy of the honor. For many, the experience is almost evangelical, as he wished it to be. Charles Fagan recalls Ralph saying to the staff on the day the Rhinelander opened its doors, "I want this to be an experience for people. If somebody is walking home and just wants to take five minutes off by coming into our store—that's how you should make people feel. The city is a really cold place and if they can come in here and have a sense of warmth, like they were in somebody's home, that's what I want to give people." Fagan remembers how struck he was with the fact that Ralph mentioned neither skirt lengths or money. Calling Ralph "the first serial shopper" and "the ultimate consumer," he maintains that the skill of the man as a retailer springs from the fact that "he always walks into every store, including his own, as a consumer. His viewpoint is always the viewpoint of a consumer. Really, he's asking, 'did it seduce me so much that I wanted to buy?'"

If Ralph Lauren's theme song should be Sinatra's "I did it my way"—and no man can make that claim with more truth than Lauren—its rider should be, "and so can you, if you do as I say." It is a question of conviction. And Ralph Lauren's conviction is total. That is why 867 Madison Avenue was such a huge success with the public, even if, as *Fortune* magazine points out, it should not have been so because it "is quite simply over the top in its Englishness, lacking only an Anglican bishop, a Simpson's meat cart and Dr. Johnson buried under the tie counter." *Fortune's* assessment was not entirely right. The store was not overtly English. It was old-world gracious and had as much in common with between-the-wars Brooks Brothers as with any shop in Jermyn Street. The staff, carefully chosen, were taught not to be servile, as the English would have been taught, but to be friendly. Today, this sort of relaxed confidence can be taken for granted but, in the mid-eighties, formality in grand shops was still the rule more often than not. The change is another example of how Ralph Lauren quietly altered the climate of the retail trade.

One of the things which intrigued all who entered the Rhinelander was the artefacts scattered throughout the store to give the effect of a family baronial hall. As with Paris, Ralph Lauren's creative staff had scoured Europe and America for props appropriate to the settings. As one wag commented at the opening, "There can't be a cricket bat left in the length and breadth of England!" A store like the Rhinelander is rather like an ocean-going liner, newly launched, arriving at the quayside. All eyes are on it, and all the other craft bobbing beside it look very small indeed. Bloomingdale's and other stores committed to Polo Ralph Lauren were nervous of its impact on their own sales. From the day of its opening millions of words were written about it and its wonders. Someone actually took the time to list them all so that customers wouldn't miss them.

He noted candles that had been lit and then snuffed so that they wouldn't look too new; the most beautiful and astonishing flowers … extreme, exotic, magnified; and "strawberries, raspberries and stuff like that served to customers from 3 to 5pm, then cocktails and canapés after 5pm." It is perhaps not surprising that a wag said, "What is this place—a store? A hotel? A home?" The answer was all three rolled into one, if you wished them to be.

It became the chic place to be seen. But, as *New York* magazine pointed out, "People have to dress for this place." The store was jam-packed with people from the moment the doors opened in the morning to closing time in the evening. Bloomingdale's executive vice president of sales tried to be philosophical, claiming that "any time you have a store of that magnitude open near you there'll be an impact," adding hopefully, "but it will begin to dissipate 30–90 days after the opening." In fact, it did and, true to Ralph Lauren's prediction, rather than take sales away from the department stores which stocked him—which was every quality store in New York—the Rhinelander actually stimulated sales and the fact that every serious shopper in the city seemingly felt that the mystical compulsion to buy into the Polo Ralph Lauren world more than justified the serious money the experience could cost them.

On the surface, 1986 appeared to be Ralph Lauren's *annus mirabilis*. The London store was his, having bought out his partner. Paris had caught the imagination of the *Bon Chic, Bon Genre* crowd. Across Europe generally the Polo look was appealing to rich international tastes in Munich, Geneva and Knocke in Belgium. But there was a shadow over the success, and it went back to 1984 when Ralph had been diagnosed as having a brain tumor. As it was not malignant, the medical decision at that point was not to operate but to monitor it. During the summer of 1986, doctors advised Ralph that the time was approaching when he must undergo surgery.

Below left and right: Outside or inside, the Chicago store is an exercise in grandeur.

Early in the new year, Ralph had a lunch appointment with his old friend and supporter Marvin Traub. As Traub recalls, the moment they took their table, he could see that Ralph was troubled. Ralph told him, "My father is in the hospital, I've just been up to see him. My brother had a stroke. And six months ago I was told that I have a brain tumor that's probably benign but needs to be operated on, and I haven't told anybody." Ralph's operation was scheduled for five days after the Fall 1987 Women's Collection show, which turned out to be a considerable commercial success.

Now Ralph had to tell his family and his closest staff. He told his teenage children informally, at the end of a family meal, taking pains to point out how routine and normal the operation was. He succeeded in downplaying the gravity of the situation so successfully that David recalls, "I never doubted that he was going to be OK. The worst part for us kids was that he was going to have his head shaved." Ricky feels that the experience had a permanent effect on her husband, claiming, "It made him more appreciative of—and more humbled and amazed at—the enormous extent of the gift he had been given. He's become more spiritual." As he recovered, colleagues also noticed a change in Ralph Lauren, "he loosened up." Ralph himself had always been a sportsman, keen on keeping fit. After the operation, fitness became more than a hobby, it developed into an obsession.

Matters of the spirit and the soul occupy Ralph Lauren a great deal. He tries to use his position of great privilege for good, either on a public or a personal level. In one sense, his whole career has been geared to doing good in that he has put into practice his belief that life could be made better for people by improving the quality of the artefacts in that life. He believed, and still does, that beauty, style and harmony all enhance life—and, of course, he is correct. But his philosophy is that the pleasures come only to those who strive for them. The work ethic is important to Lauren. He sees it as crucial to man's need to aspire, to prove and to improve himself. It is an effective equation for all its simplicity: if you work hard and are lucky, you can have what you aspire to, and enjoy it because it is earned.

Ralph Lauren's accumulation of wealth, and the lifestyle that comes with it, is often confused with snobbery by commentators. They link it with the vignettes he creates in his advertising campaigns of English country houses between the wars or the American upper classes from the Gilded Age. But Lauren's fascination with the privileged life is nothing to do with exclusivity. It is to do with the wellspring of all that he does. It is about perfection. Getting it right and making it the best is his credo. He will not cut corners and he will never accept second best. That is why he sets out to recreate the upper classes in their brief modern moment of glory. To him, they and their relaxed confidence were the best, whether it is manifested in the sophistication of a simple, perfectly cut and virtually unadorned silk dress or the subversive casualness of cricket trousers held up by an old school tie, left dangling at the hip. Whether the day was casual or smart, the evening was always correct—and so it is in a Lauren advertisement: the men's black ties just might be undone at the end of the evening but the dinner jacket will still show its perfect cut; the women's dresses will be simple and unassuming but of the very highest quality and, even after dinner, backgammon and possibly some impromptu dancing, the expensively styled hair will still fall perfectly into place.

Elegance, undemonstrative but evident, is in Ralph Lauren's opinion the thing which brings style.

Elegance, undemonstrative but evident, is in Ralph Lauren's opinion the thing which brings style. That is why he chose Polo as the sport which would sum up his approach. There is, after all, nothing more elegant than a well-bred and perfectly groomed horse, unless it is the long-legged hound which has traditionally accompanied it. Human beings are greatly enhanced by the horse— as Diana Vreeland's 1984 exhibition at the Metropolitan Museum of Art, titled with devastatingly direct simplicity, "Man and the Horse"—set out to prove. It seems entirely appropriate that the man whose logo is a polo player should be the sponsor of the show. Vreeland's horse was a fashion item. To an extent, it also is for Lauren. He associates horses with the swank of perfection that he finds in the beautiful woman, with long legs, well-groomed hair and the fresh, fit look that American women have above all others—thoroughbreds like "Babe" Paley and CZ Guest. In fact, the personification of the Lauren vision of perfection—cool but also warm, dignified but capable of fun.

All the rich and beautiful in the fifties—Paley, Guest or Mona Bismark—were, in effect, film stars without a screen. Endlessly photographed by the likes of Beaton and Horst, the perfection of their appearance rivaled that of any screen goddess. Where did the young Ralph Lauren learn about such female types but at the movies, where all the stars were elegant. Like millions of young men, he fell in love with the quick-witted, emancipated characters played by Katharine Hepburn, dressed in perfectly cut pants and a cashmere sweater. It was the simplicity—an essentially American, sporting, outdoor girl simplicity—which gave a woman like Katharine Hepburn not only her sex appeal but also her class. There was no vulgar "money on legs" feeling about her. Money was just incidental. The same went for Hollywood's other variations on the sexy woman with class, Carole Lombard, Greer Garson, Lauren Bacall and, in the fifties and sixties, their modern counterparts, pre-eminently Grace Kelly and Audrey Hepburn, who could never be called anything as crass as sex symbols. Their sexual appeal was about allure, something very much more subtle.

If these were the dream girls for many men, Ralph Lauren can be said to have found his own version of their screen perfection in Ricky Lowbeer. Refined, ladylike, delicate, she is everything a Lauren woman should be. The family are the reality of the Lauren dream come true. In fact, it is probably true to say that they are the template for the looks, as well as the advertisements, which have made Ralph Lauren famous. The boys are darkly handsome, Dylan is animated and pretty. All three are the antithesis of the "spoilt brat" children of rich and important parents. As a family they stand as the living example of all that Ralph Lauren dreamed of and everything in which he believes. They are the ones he is clothing every time he creates a collection. They are the ones whose needs he considers with each new range. They are also the ones with whom he talks, keeping in touch with the lifestyle of the young; testing his fashion ideas against theirs and catching the mood of the moment through the movies and the music that they enjoy. One of Ralph Lauren's great strengths as a designer is the fact that he has this informal and unofficial family team to keep him aware and attuned to the world of the young. In this he is almost unique; few designers are married with children, especially at that cutting-edge age when they are part of the boiling cauldron of fad, fancy and fashion which makes for the feeling of "now".

Early in their childhood, Ralph, who has always chased the eternal bluebird of youth, decided that his children would grow up to be his friends. He has achieved that goal with spectacular success. As his eldest child, Andrew, expresses it, "My father always played the role of a regular father. Far from being the man who never came to dinner, he was always there for dinner so we shared a lot of our youth with him. He was never a stranger coming home. I give him great credit for being able to play the father role when he was under the stress of developing a company." Born when his father was not famous and growing up with that fame, Andrew is like his mother in having to change and adjust as the social position of the family altered. He confesses, "It was always an odd feeling to walk down the street and suddenly see somebody wearing my father's work. You see this horse with a guy on it and somebody is wearing it, like a piece of artwork or something. I remember when I was about 11 cutting out pictures from magazines of dad wearing a horse or the Kennedys wearing a horse and seeing my name in the papers. But even then I think I knew my father might well be a public man but that he was actually a private—a very private—man. He and my mother were very protective of us. They wanted us to be low-key so that we could have a normal childhood and we remained that way for a long time. My memory of my dad is not of a guy who was famous but the person who I wrestled and ran around with when I was a kid."

Ralph Lauren didn't leave his work behind at the office. Andrew recalls how his father would bring home advertising campaigns or show him a model and ask for his opinion. Charles Fagan points out that, in his work, Ralph "listens a lot and asks questions." He also guides people. One of his commonest expressions is "just ask me." David Lauren remembers that, "My dad very rarely came home and talked about business problems but he educated us from when we were very little about everything he was doing. Even when I was about five years old, he'd say, 'David, should we buy this house?' We had very serious debates. He would bring home clothes and say, 'Do you like this sweater?' He would take our advice like we were one of his consumers. He listened to everything and dissected it. So, when I went to school, I never really thought of my dad as anything special. He was just my dad. Special to me was if I was on a team or involved in some office in student government. I kind of knew his significance because when we grew we saw his name everywhere. He was always around, in every sense."

Ralph Lauren worked at nourishing friendship with his children, determined to remain a part of their lives. No matter how busy, if one of them phoned him at work he would always pick up the phone. David says, "I spent a lot of time growing up with him, after school. I would ask him questions about girls and he would ask me questions about school. It seems he was always there." Not only was he there, he did what all parents do, in that, even when his children were young he wanted them to share his enthusiasms as much as he was eager to share theirs. His daughter Dylan was, like her brothers, involved in sport from an early age, running and playing basketball with the boys, cycling with her mother and father. She remembers the days they spent on Long Island in the summers of their childhood when her father would orchestrate the whole day into things the children would enjoy doing—but always things in which he and Ricky could share. The ethos was of a fit healthy family emotionally attuned. Andrew remembers that the structure of discipline which underpinned daily life was provided by his mother, who hated it when the children quarreled. "My mom can wear the pants a lot. My dad is more passive but he was always there to defend my mom. If we did something wrong, he would get angry," David says. "He only really lost his temper if we kids were being mean to each other. He'd come in and say, 'What do you guys think you're doing?' He never took sides. I guess he was pretty even-tempered."

Above left and right: Rooms within
rooms in the Chicago store.

Above: A gentleman's club atmosphere recreated for the Chicago store.

Ralph Lauren has created a vast empire that rests on his name. It would be expected that he would wish it to be carried on by one, or all, of his children, but he has never put any overt pressure on them to come into the business. Andrew, who works as an actor and producer in the feature film business, believes that he and his father are too close in personality to really work together. Dylan also feels that her world is elsewhere. She and her business partner are already running a hugely successful retail empire of themed candy stores called Dylan's Candy Bar. In a close-knit family, however, it is inevitable that the fashion input that Ralph Lauren receives from his children is considerable, if casual. They bring to Ralph a vital awareness of what is happening within their age band. Informal, unofficial style counsellors is perhaps the best role that the children can play in their father's business. For example, when Ralph Lauren was asked to make a guest appearance on the TV program *Friends* (Jennifer Aniston's character Rachel is employed at Ralph Lauren as a designer)—one of his favorite shows—there was much family discussion. To begin with he was doubtful, Dylan says, but once they had persuaded him that "it would be a smart PR move," he went in wholeheartedly.

The only one of the children who has joined Polo Ralph Lauren is David. His interest is in communication rather than design—he started his own magazine when he was still at college and it flourished. Putting Polo on the Internet was his first responsibility and it would seem that he will be part of the organization on a permanent basis. Charles Gwathmay believes that Ralph finds this to be most satisfying and reassuring, both in terms of the Polo legacy, as well as familial continuity. Ralph and David communicate. There is no question that David's intuition and instincts are totally supportive and unconflicted. In Ricky, he has the perfect alter dresser. She is an integral part of his/Polo's image. What she wears, how she looks—and how she wants to look—are of vital importance to Ralph. She is much more than a muse—she is his ultimate model. Ralph is a wonderfully supportive father on all levels. His children are both extensions of his life and vision, as well as individuals whom he wants to succeed in their own right. However, deep down, I believe, if they were all someday involved with the company, if would be his ultimate satisfaction."

The fact remains that the key element is still Ralph Lauren himself, rather than the family he has so assiduously kept out of the limelight. How much does the image of masculinity, which his products project, reflect Ralph Lauren himself? What manner of man is the Ralph Lauren man? Above all, what are his antecedents?

The Ralph Lauren man can be traced to more than one source. Like a river and its tributaries, some are stronger than others. The power that drives them all is Ralph's belief that the elegant man does not always have to be the cultured, city sophisticate. For him, elegance springs from attitude of mind. He has no doubt that the figure created by physical exercise is the modern figure, whether it belongs to an accountant or a cowboy. He is also sure that the modern man is the fit man. In Ralph Lauren's lexicon of style, there is really no place for the flabbily overweight. Suave and svelte in a Purple Label suit, or lean and work-honed in jeans and plaid shirt, the masculinity of the Lauren man springs from the fact that he is in shape—whether as a result of days spent in the saddle or hours at the gym. His voice is measured and controlled and yet it is apparent that he is a man of action, decisive, determined and a natural leader. In movie terms, it is the serious, thoughtful man of the plains whose solitude has given him strength of character. This is, to a point, a description of Ralph Lauren. Quiet-tongued, moving like a cowboy, he also has the natural authority of the born leader.

It is no secret that Ralph Lauren's stimulation is largely visual. It is also no secret that when he was young the movies were his obsession. He has explained many times that they were not an escape for him. They were a path to a reality that he was determined would be his, full of the romance that goes with glamor. Many people have speculated over the possibility of Ralph Lauren in Hollywood. They frequently suggest that his need to control would have led him toward production or direction. That reflects today's Ralph Lauren, the head of the company. In fact, his early years in the tie business demonstrate that he was a showman as much as a salesman. Surely, if he was not born to be an actor, he certainly was brought up to be the center of admiration, both in and out of home.

Searching for a role model, as young men do, he looked to movie stars. The world he saw was the world of Randolph Scott, steel-eyed and uncompromisingly honorable, the quintessential cowboy, or that of James Stewart or Cary Grant, the master of social aplomb. Later there would be Frank Sinatra, Paul Newman, James Dean: Ralph Lauren learned something from them all. Above all, he learned what the good actor must learn, control of himself, his space and his audience. He has honed the skills to a fine point where, softly spoken, he never fails to command attention.

Sport, his other obsession, would have been his first choice of career, were it not demolished by his lack of height. Again, such an ambition reflects the desire to be a hero and the wish for that heroism to be based on physical prowess. It is something ingrained in the male psyche and goes back to the days of the gladiators, Condottieri, and the Landsknecht, the hired mercenaries who swaggered across medieval Europe with their clothes provocatively torn in order to demonstrate their contempt for ordered society.

Lauren combines the sportsman's precise eye with the cowboy's ability to take in the bigger vista along with the incidentals. As Bruce Weber points out, Lauren's eye "doesn't just notice things but connects them." It is this connecting thread which makes Ralph Lauren's retail stores, once described as "houses with everything but a kitchen," such a powerful part of the vision. Uniquely, perhaps, their main purpose is not necessarily to make money. It has been generally accepted since its opening that the Rhinelander loses money. Appropriately known within the Lauren organization as the Mansion, its losses were calculated in 1998 by the *Chicago Tribune* to even top as much as $1 million per month. Lauren's riposte was revealing: "You don't open up anything not to be moneymakers, but what the Madison Avenue store has done is to make a lot more money for the company anyway. People come in and maybe they don't buy something then, but they buy something of mine later, somewhere else. What it does for the overall picture is it sets the tone."

As the Polo Ralph Lauren organization has expanded, the tone has broadened. The overall retail concept has not changed but it has been used flexibly in order that local stores, whilst always being instantly recognizable by ambience and mood to be Polo outlets, display a degree of personality that fits both location and clientele. The original London store had its own individuality but nobody who entered it once it had become a Lauren outlet could ever mistake it for anything other than a Polo Ralph Lauren shop. Partly this is due to the merchandise and the way it is displayed but is also the result of careful scene dressing in order that the shop looks "lived in." As Charles Fagan explains it: "With everything in Polo Ralph Lauren there is an overall sense of a vernacular, a spirit, a sensibility but there is a range within that allows a certain freedom. As in the

He creates shops which marry form and function in
a way that the customer can understand so that they feel
good, they're relaxed and the experience is a positive one.

The original Ralph Lauren London store in Bond Street, now
devoted entirely to children's clothing.

clothes. Ralph is always inspired by function. Design frivolity is repellent to him. He creates shops which marry form and function in a way that the customer can understand so that they feel good, they're relaxed and the experience is a positive one. There is a quality, an emotion and a balance in his stores."

Whether a store is in Beverley Hills, Chicago or Phoenix, the concept is always present, although even that, according to Fagan, is changing. "Today," he says, "we're opening stores which are smaller, tighter and more focussed to the needs of a particular community and attempting less to give the entire world of Ralph Lauren. There's so much now, it's almost impossible to put it all under one roof without destroying the quality of intimacy, of Ralph Lauren talking directly to you, the customer, which must always be preserved because that is what it is all about. We want to send a message that's connected with where the store is. The Soho store is entirely different from the Mansion. In Palm Beach the sensibility of the store is very much the Duke and Duchess of Windsor. Beverley Hills is Hollywood-geared. The country store in East Hampton is casual and eclectic, which is exactly what the Hamptons are about." All of which is true, but the Lauren mood is pre-eminently about a certain monumentality, as in the Chicago store, opening in November 1998—at 37,000 square feet of retail space, the largest of all Ralph Lauren's stores. Located on Michigan Avenue, in the city's heartland for high-quality shopping, the store represented an extension to the Lauren vision, since it housed the first Ralph Lauren restaurant. Called simply RL and capable of seating 98 diners, it has all the Lauren trademarks: mahogany paneling, leather banquettes, lights found in a British railway station waiting room, classic black and white images of Hollywood's greats and select artwork acquired from the archives of The Chicago Historical Society covering the walls. "Just as retailing is a moving concept," Ralph explained to local journalists, "with people going to stores because they want the product, so it's also a form of entertainment, of getting a mood. I've often wished I could go to a restaurant which was like one of my stores and could keep the mood going. This restaurant is based on the kind of place I would like to go." It also has the sort of menu Ralph Lauren likes and it features steaks sourced on the Double RL ranch in Colorado.

Six months later, in May 1999, Ralph Lauren opened a new store in London, at Number 1 New Bond Street, to replace his original store which, grown inadequate to house all the merchandise, became his first free-standing children's store. Designed by the self-styled "eclectic classicist", New York-based French architect Thierry Despont, its 45,000 square feet, of which 24,000 are for retail, the rest being offices, were designed to evoke the feeling of one of the great transatlantic liners of the past, specifically *The Normandie*, possibly the most fashionable and certainly the best designed of any of the big boats of the twenties. Dupont wished to create an atmosphere "both exciting and elegant, like being invited for a drink in a great club in Hollywood or London in the early thirties." In keeping with the mood, the pre-opening night party was one of the most glittering for a Ralph Lauren store. Guests included the Duke of York, Carolyn Bessette Kennedy and John F. Kennedy jr., along with members of the British aristocracy and establishment figures from London and America.

Lauren felt strongly that the new London store should speak of Ralph Lauren *per se* rather than of Ralph Lauren bringing back to London its own values. Tactfully, he and his architect have

selling the dream **153**

avoided accusations of "bringing coals to Newcastle" by playing down the English feeling which permeates the Rhinelander mansion. Light mahogany is as much in evidence as dark. Steel takes the place of brass. Suede seating based on twenties' originals replaces the more usual copies of eighteenth-century club chairs. Black-and-white pictures of jazz players, Clark Gable and Jimmy Stewart decorate the walls. As Ralph Lauren said, "I love the warmth of a club, but with glamor and quality. I feel that this is a new step for us, a movement that just feels right."

It is this feeling for "rightness," almost always infallible because totally instinctive, which had earlier moved Lauren into a retail area which surprised many. The Polo Sport store, opened in 1993, exactly opposite the Mansion, forced all those who felt that Lauren had become so formulaic that he was in danger of trapping himself in a sort of atavistic sterility to rethink. As always with Lauren, it was a change in merchandise that heralded a broadened approach, the necessity for a store only becoming apparent to many observers after its opening. In fact, the store had been in Lauren's mind for some time. As a committed sportsperson and aficionado of the gymnasium, he had realized that the use of leisure time for sport was one of the great retail growth areas. As he told *The New York Times*, "The fashion of the nineties is about health. And when I say health, I don't mean doctors. I mean body consciousness, consciousness of eating the right foods, throwing away the junk foods, feeling good on the inside and looking it on the outside. Everyone goes to spas; everyone seems to have a trainer, or they're running or working out in a gym."

The interior of the store, realized by the architect Richard Gould, was subtle, sophisticated and essentially modern. But, like all of Lauren's interiors, it was not starkly so. Nor was it so of the moment that it could date. Instead, it was based on the architecture of Walter Gropius and Le Corbusier; the photographs of Horst, Hoynigan-Huene and Munkacsi. White lacquered walls, cherry wood floors and stainless steel give a feeling of efficiency without sacrificing warmth. It has been described as being "as clean as a baseball," acknowledging the functionalism of the approach although, as with all Lauren stores, props abound in order to set the mood. The "Great Outdoors" is invoked by canoes and kayaks fixed to the walls. A racing scull is suspended from the ceiling. Vintage skiing posters and a bank of video screens broaden the mood. It is a modern temple to the godlike sportsman from a man "inspired," as Charles Fagan puts it, "by heroes." As with the Rhinelander, Fagan recalls that many inside the firm felt that "to take a store that size might prove not to be the smartest business decision but Ralph had made up his mind to send a message saying, "I am moving. I am not sedentary. I do clothes which are authentic and this is my statement." It was a move which changed a lot of perceptions of what Ralph is and helped people see that he wasn't just that WASP, English-inspired thing."

This ability to capture the present and yet project into the future in a way that so convinces people that they wish to go with him is, in the opinion of Rob Frieda, the bedrock of Ralph Lauren's genius as a creator and retailer. "I think it is easy to forget," he warns, "that Ralph was a complete pioneer, not least in the marketing area. He virtually created environmental marketing, which is the strategic development of a demand for a product by associating the brand name with certain desires within the market. The skill, of course, is to spot the desire before anybody else. Ralph's a genius at it. What he did was to take not only the brand creation at the strategic level but he then translated that through environmental marketing so that when customers actually came into the space it was as reflective of the overall image of the brand as the advertising was. Ralph didn't get lucky with the WASP aspiration. He hit right on the wave front and capitalized on it. He knew what the market needed then and he knows what the market needs now. That is the quintessence of his success. He has a fantastically flexible mind." What Frieda could have added is that, not only flexible, the mind is always looking ahead anticipating developments and evolving future strategies. Wishing to raise the profile of his menswear in Europe, Ralph decided to open offices and showrooms in Milan's via San Barnaba. Opulent, elegant, the Lauren Palazzo has the characteristics which bespeak Polo Ralph Lauren: wood panelling, antique rugs, bookcases and that air of calm confidence which permeates all the company's buildings. He, in January 2002, the exlusive Ralph Lauren Purple Label menswear collection was shown to a small audience of the world's top fashion editors. Its huge success was echoed five months later, with the second Purple Label show in Milan. Ralph told a press conference "I wanted to make a statement about the level of quality and sophistcation in American fashion. For twenty years the Lauren dream had been hung on the shoulders of elegant, assured and fit-looking models, all of whom were beautiful in a classic, understated way."

The Milan move was an example of Ralph Lauren's ability to adapt and expand the perception of his labels. If Europe had seen his contribution as sporty, casual wear, the formality of Purple Label changed that idea for good. It was the sort of bold, not entirely expected, but totally correct, change of emphasis which had led Ralph, in 1994, to employ a new model who dramatically affected how the Polo brand was perceived, by modernising and broadening its image.

Within the next two years, that changed—not, according to Pat Christman, from any outside pressure or desire to milk a new market but simply because Ralph suddenly saw the perfect man

Below: The new London store.

to personify the image of Polo Sport. His color, she maintains, was not a serious consideration. "Ralph just thought Tyson was a great-looking guy," she says. Tyson Beckford was certainly that but Weber believes that Ralph deserves more credit for using a black model for advertisements which, even in the early nineties, were still more likely to pull in white customers than those from ethnic groups. "Ralph knew Tyson was right for the moment," he insists, "But it was quite a thing for Ralph to do. He used Tyson because he believed in his look, not because he felt he would sell more clothes. I think it was really great that Ralph took such a strong stand." Tyson has a fine physique. Many models, regardless of color, have the same. What made him different was his face, which was an archetype of handsomeness that appealed to people of all colors. Although born in America, he was brought up in Jamaica and feels that his features are the result of a Chinese grandmother and a Panamanian grandfather on his mother's side. He was used in a Polo Sport advertisement in 1994 and was signed to an exclusive contract the next year not only because, in Lauren's view, he had "that all-American look." Tyson's appeal, to the public as well as to Ralph Lauren, was based on the fact that he was the embodiment of male power in its modern form. Unsmiling, gazing into the far distance, he was the urban equivalent of that archetype of American masculinity, the cowboy.

One of the things associated with the sportsman is the freedom that traditionally cowboys have been romantically considered to possess. Although in physical terms, it had no more meaning than the fact that they were paid to cover considerable distances, it might be true that long hours alone could create a feeling of freedom in the mind of a cowboy. Surfers, climbers and other obsessional sportsmen would claim the same. The dream of self-sufficiency, the hope of avoiding responsibilities and the belief in finding oneself by turning away from society have probably been

Previous page: Purple Label menswear.
Pages 156 and 157: Spring 2003.

Right: The menswear department of the London store.

talismen of the young male for many generations. It was the film *Easy Rider* that linked them with the motorbike, the modern equivalent of the cowboy's horse. Virtually every young man of spirit dreams at one time or another of that hallowed combination of machine, man and universe which was given almost mystic meaning by Robert M Pirsig's *Zen and the Art of Motorcycle Maintenance*, a book which Ralph Lauren found as moving as the novels of Jack Kerouac. David Lauren tells how, inadvertently, he was the instrument that made it possible for his father to rekindle a portion of youth. "I would like to take credit for the fact that my dad is now into motorbikes," he says. "I wanted to buy a motorbike but he and my mom were really not happy about it. So, I took him to the motorcycle store and, after we looked at them, he said 'all right!' I couldn't decide between a red one or a yellow one and whilst I was still deliberating he said to me one day when we were in Seattle, 'You get the red one; I'll get the yellow one.' That's how it started. Then he took it onto a completely new level by buying a Ducatti." Ralph Lauren did not just buy the Ducatti, he customized it, virtually redesigning the bike in silver aluminium to make his own statement. "So," David laughs, "what started as a relaxing, freedom sort of thing has become a hobby so absorbing that we go to motorcycle stores whenever we can and talk about all the utilities. It's very much a bonding thing. We bought bikes on the same day and we ride together. I would literally rush up to Bedford to go riding with my dad. So, then my mom didn't want to be left out, so she took motorcycle lessons, although I don't think she's going to pursue it."

Ralph Lauren's love of elegance and speed has always been associated with motorcars and they are still an over-riding passion. He never merely bought a car. He always bought a vehicle which, for him, had an aura and history which lifted it above the merely mechanical. He always knew which cars to buy, having learned of their importance as part of the projected image even when he was a youth in the Bronx. And he learned it from the movies. Cary Grant and Grace Kelly driving along the Corniche above Nice in an open tourer inspired his lifelong devotion to British and Continental sportscars. The dream began to become reality, Ralph claims, when his brother returned from his military service in Germany. "He came back with some money and he bought himself a little MG. I had just turned eighteen. My brother was a good guy; very occasionally he would lend me his car." When Ralph had done his military service, he repeated the pattern, investing his first savings in a 1961 Morgan, although it was not in good condition. It cost him $1,600—and he loved it. "It was a dream come true," he claims. "It was one of those beautiful Indian summer days in November when I bought it. I put the top down, slid into the driver's seat and took off. I was 22 years old. It was my first car. I never dreamed of a Ferrari. I had never even seen one. I was in love with my Morgan and that was enough." Sadly, it broke down once too often, when he and Ricky were visiting friends in Connecticut. The friends bought it and the pair returned to New York by bus, but the car was dear to their hearts and they later repurchased it. They have it still.

Ralph claims never to have set out to build up his unbeatable collection of automobiles. "I'm not really a collector," he insists. "But I have always loved beauty, quality, and genuineness in any object. I'm drawn to the combination of advanced technology and the romance of the past. It's not unusual for a young man in America to grow up car crazy. As kids, my friends and I would count the cars that went by: 'Look, there goes a Pontiac; there's an Olds; here's a Cadillac.'" From

Ralph Lauren has always looked for ways in which to sponsor activities which make Americans aware of their past and give them pride in their present.

car spotting to building up a collection of some of the world's most magnificent cars has taken Ralph Lauren a lifetime. Each one is unique, from his 1929 4.5 super-charged Bentley to his collection of twelve red Ferraris. His first Ferrari was a 1971 Daytona Spyder, followed by a 278 GTB-4, a model of which less than a dozen survive today. "By then I was hooked," Ralph told *Ferrari* magazine in 1990. "I went after what most people consider the ultimate Ferrari—a GTO. There were about three dozen of these cars made by Ferrari and they are so rare that dealers keep careful track of owners who get divorced or run into business setbacks and have to sell. I've had mine since 1986." Bugatti Atlantic … Alfa Romeo 2900 … Mercedes SSK … the Lauren collection is a rollcall of honor of everything for which elegant, individual machines can stand but it also includes a US-army jeep, a much-loved "woody" and, in Colorado, an old Ford pick-up truck for which Ralph bargained a long time before persuading its owner to part with it. "Each one has its own distinctive character," he claims. "And I love driving them all. The sportscars are the most exciting pieces of art I know and I think of them as athletes—they need a workout every so often or they get sick. And driving them is a workout for me, too. Each car is a new experience, a means of expression." As he wrote in *Art and Antiques* of March 1991, "There's nothing like waking up on a nice sunny morning, putting on a hat and goggles, rolling down the top of a convertible and putting it through a few paces on a country road. The pleasure I get is not about trying to go fast; it's the feeling of handling a thoroughbred: the way it comes around a corner; the way the mechanism feels when you shift. The engine is roaring and your heart is pounding. It's one of life's true pleasures."

Such a comment sums up Ralph Lauren for what many friends feel he is: a frustrated man of action who requires a physical challenge and even a degree of danger. For him, the visual and tactile impact of a hand-made car designed by one of the world's great automobile specialists is as valid a form of art as a piece of sculpture. Lauren has often been criticized for what is perceived as a narrow range of cultural interests. He admits that, unlike Ricky, he is not a reader, something he regrets. "I wish I read more," he says, "but I can't sit still and concentrate for long enough. I need to be doing something physical, even if it is just playing ping pong with the kids."

Ralph Lauren has always supported philanthropic activities which make Americans aware of their past and give them pride in their present. Like all corporations which donate considerable amounts of money to worthy causes, Polo Ralph Lauren wishes to gain benefits through association in whatever enterprise they choose to back. For example Polo Ralph Lauren sponsorsed Diana Vreeland's "Man and the Horse" exhibition at the Metropolitan Museum. The company has given financial backing to various other exhibitions of American art over the years. In appreciation of his support, The Museum of American Folk Art honored Ralph at a benefit dinner in 1988 to mark the opening of "Folk Art of the Westward Movement," which he curated. The citations made clear the important role of Polo Ralph Lauren in making Americans aware of their culture. The evening's program noted how Lauren "inspired by the extraordinary history of American creative expression, has helped secure an international audience and appreciation of our national heritage." Nancy Reagan, writing from the White House as Honorary Chairman, pointed out Lauren's importance as an American fashion designer, writing of the fact that, "In his own special way [Ralph Lauren] has brought American fashion to pre-eminence around the globe," adding, "In his wonderfully generous and productive life, Ralph has made an indelible imprint on the fashion world. His designs reflect the true spirit of our great land. I am honored to join you in thanking Ralph for his contribution to American style, and I am proud to call him my friend."

The arts of America must include film and it is not surprising that a man who had so many of his dreams formed by Hollywood, whose friends include stars like Woody Allen, Robert Redford, Barbra Streisand and Audrey Hepburn, would wish to be involved with the medium. Polo Ralph Lauren encouraged young film makers through its sponsorship of the Columbia University Film Festival and awarded prizes for the Best Film, Best Comedy and Best Screenplay. It also gave a development grant to further young talent. Telluride residents, Ralph and Ricky Lauren, have underwritten the festival's outdoor cinema for 18 years. The annual Telluride Film Festival is seen by many as a non-commercial alternative to the Sundance Festival. Polo Ralph Lauren's involvement grew over the years and they are now the presenting sponsor of the four-day festival.

In addition to the charities and good causes to which Ralph Lauren anonymously gives his own money, Polo Ralph Lauren devotes funds publicly to certain philanthropic concerns. His commitment to the fight against cancer goes back for over a decade. In the early eighties he was co-founder, with Katharine Graham of the Nina Hyde Center for Breast Cancer Research at Georgetown University, Washington D.C. Ralph admired Nina professionally—she was the fashion editor of the *Washington Post*—and he admired her courage in the face of her illness even more. Hyde herself said "He really committed himself." His speech at a fundraising event where the pair shared a platform was a reminder that Ralph, who never reads a prepared speech or uses notes, has a natural and informal ability with words. "I told them", he recalls "I know that if you're sick in a hospital—as popular and as strong as you are—you are alone. You are sitting in a little room, and you're scared and you're wearing some funny pyjamas they gave you. And you want someone to visit you. I say we should always remember these moments. We have to take care of people."

In 1996 he was co-host, with Anna Wintour, editor-in-chief of American *Vogue*, of a charity gala "Salute to American Fashion" held in Washington to raise funds with the Princess of Wales as honorary chair for the evening. That night Ralph said "Breast cancer is not just a women's issue. It affects all of us; the brothers, fathers, husbands, children and friends of the women who are dealing with the disease."

Ralph also designed the logo for the Council of Fashion Designers of America's "Fashion Targets Breast Cancer" campaign. First presented in the United States in 1994, the campaign now covers Australia, Brazil, Canada, Great Britain and Greece and has raised over $20 million. Ralph Lauren's commitment to cancer charities has deepened over the years. Polo Ralph Lauren gave a $6 million leadership grant to establish the Ralph Lauren Center for Cancer Care and Prevention, to meet the needs of low-income patients in Harlem and offers screening, research and treatment within the community. In September 2000, he launched the Pink Pony Campaign, to raise both funds, and international awareness in order to provide cancer care in medically deprived areas. In spring 2001, the Pink Pony T-shirt was introduced. It became an international "must have" within the fashion world.

Perhaps Polo Ralph Lauren's greatest act of charity was the donation of $13 million ($10 million in cash and $3 million in pro-bono advertising support) to the Smithsonian's American Museum of Natural History Institute in Washington for the preservation of the Star Spangled Banner. It was as much an emotional decision as it was a shrewd corporate move. The short statement Polo Ralph Lauren released pointed out that "The flag is an inspiration for all Americans and it captures the dreams and imaginations of men and women all over the world. I am a product of the American dream and the flag is its symbol." At the ceremony and news conference held on July 13, 1998 at the Smithsonian, President Clinton and Hillary Rodham Clinton stood next to Ralph and, surrounded by children symbolizing the future, recited the Pledge of Allegiance before the Star Spangled Banner. In his address, President Clinton commented, "You know, most of us have—well, maybe not most of us but a lot of us, including Hillary and me—have those great Polo sweaters with the American flag on them. I wish I had one with the Star Spangled Banner on it because that's the gift that he's given America today." The First Lady pointed out that, when he had heard of the state of the Star Spangled Banner, Ralph had just "picked up the phone" and talked to her, explaining that "he was blessed by our nation and wanted to give something back." She then went on to add what, for the Lauren organization, was the dream comment: "The phrase 'Ralph Lauren' has sort of become an adjective. When you say something is very Ralph Lauren it means it has a certain American style or design. Perhaps after today it will also come to symbolize another aspect of the American way: good citizenship." Press comment on the night was generally positive, echoing the Clinton line of praise for an act of philanthropy, but no one underestimated the huge publicity that the move brought to the Polo Ralph Lauren organization. *The New York Times* made the point that, "For a mere $13 million—given by his corporation—Mr Lauren received an avalanche of publicity." *The Washington Post* agreed, taking the wide view that the gift showed how brand-name philanthropy "has grown by leaps and bounds as the traditional sources of funding weaken and… taboos against corporate labeling lapse."

Like every other American citizen, Ralph Lauren was deeply affected by the events of September 11th 2001. Within days of the outrage, the American Heroes Fund of the Polo Ralph Lauren Foundation was set up to enable Polo's 10,000 employees world-wide, as well as, customers and business partners, to participate in the relief efforts. The company matched employee contributions, dollar for dollar, as well as donating 10% of customer purchases from Ralph Lauren stores and as Polo.com during October 2001. The Polo Ralph Lauren Foundation's $4 million American Heroes Fund has benefited various charities set up in the aftermath of the disaster, including scholarships for the children of victim's of the attacks. The American Heroes Scholarship programs will continue for twenty years, in order that victim's children born even after the event will be eligible for scholarships.

Praise and respect have been given to Ralph Lauren from many quarters and on several levels but perhaps the most significant for him personally, as well as his corporation, have been the honors he has received from the American fashion industry itself. The list is long and impressive, beginning with The Coty American Fashion Critics' Award in 1970. He went on to win it another six times. He is the only designer to have received the Council of Fashion Designers of America's three highest honors: the Womenswear Designer of the Year Award, which was presented to him in 1996; the Menswear Designer of the Year Award, which he received in the following year. Both followed what many of those closest to him in the Ralph Lauren organization believe is the honor which means more to him personally than anything else: the CFDA Lifetime Achievement Award.

He received this honor, the highest the US fashion industry can bestow, in 1991, the star-studded presentation ceremony taking place on February 4, 1992. To Ralph's great delight, it was presented to him by a woman whom he had admired for many years. Audrey Hepburn, looking the epitome of Ralph Lauren chic, presented it to him with a speech she had personally written. *The New York Times* commented that the speech had a sort of "Holly Golightly enchantment and was delivered with harrowingly perfect diction." In her speech she commended Ralph for "always reminding us of the best things in life. As a designer you conjure up all the things I most care about: the country, misty mornings, summer afternoons, great open spaces, horses, cornfields, vegetable gardens, fireplaces and Jack Russell terriers. As a man, I respect you for your total lack of pretension, and your gentleness, kindness, sincerity and simplicity. As my friend, I love you." She then went on to elaborate on what she felt was the true achievement of Ralph Lauren, pointing out that, in her view, he had given American design a distinctive point of view and a dignity, adding, "if you say something is very Ralph Lauren, you'll be immediately understood."

Ralph's reply was extemporary. Asking for the house lights to be raised so that he could see his audience, he pointed down to his friend Steve Bell and said, putting his arm around Audrey Hepburn, "Steve, remember we went to the movies in the Bronx 30 years ago? Remember the princess? I got her." In his speech, he touched on the pressures which never lift: "You can never carry what you had yesterday with you, every show you do is a new ball game. No one cares about what you did yesterday. It's tomorrow." Talking of his early years when he was designing and selling ties, he claimed, "It was a commitment to myself, a commitment to do what I loved and to do it the best I can." It was a speech and an evening in which his friends felt he relaxed and let the world see a little more of him than he normally did; most of them agreed that the strongest impression they were left with was his quiet passion for his work and a compassion for those who had helped him achieve so much.

Compassion is not always considered a characteristic of great achievers. There is a generally held opinion that the climb to the top hardens the individual and deadens his sensitivities, leaving him self-involved and determined to have his own way. There is clearly some truth in this and yet one of the most frequent comments made about Ralph Lauren by those who really know him is that, although accepted to be driven to do it his way—to be, in the modern parlance, a control freak—he always has time to listen, and also to ask. Those who have known and worked for Ralph for any length of time contrast the atmosphere of 650 Madison with that found in the headquarters of other successful designers. As one ex-Lauren employee puts it, "He always seems to see you, unlike so many designers, who are so self-absorbed they walk straight past you. He always has time for a word or a smile and, for that reason, he is adored. He's always notoriously late for meetings. Everybody waits for the phone call saying 'Ralph is on his way.'"

As a man of considerable, if understated dignity, he respects the dignity of those who work for him. As a journalist once said of him, "The two outstanding instincts that govern Ralph Lauren's life are to be kind and in control." Edgar Bronfman, describing his first few meetings with Ralph, before the two men became friends, says that he was surprised to find that Ralph was "much more introspective, much more inclined to listen and very much warmer than I expected. He has a compassion about him." Bette-Ann Gwathmey, vice president of corporate philanthropy and a close friend of the Laurens recalls when Ralph and Ricky chaired a fundraising gala for the Robert Steel Foundation, named in honor of Bette-Ann's courageous and inspiring eighteen year-old son,

Above: Ricky and Dylan wearing Pink Pony T-shirts.

Above left: Ralph and Ricky at the CFDA award ceremony.
Above right: Audrey Hepburn presents Ralph Lauren with the CFDA Lifetime Achievement Award.

Robby, who lost his battle with cancer in 1984. "It was the world's premier of the film *The Firm* at Bryant Park. The park was aglow with thousands of candles, beautiful flowers and white umbrellas. Ralph and Ricky's generosity as well as their tremendous kindness was so evident that night—it was infectious. The event was an enormous success, raising over a million dollars for pediatric cancer research. I will alway be grateful to Ralph and Ricky for their leadership and their compassion." There are other stories of his practical generosity: the occasion when he bought a car for a janitor's son who had only a limited time to live; the way in which he put his plane at the disposal of a member of his staff in Jamaica who needed to be flown to New York for treatment; the employee in Colorado whose medical treatment he took care of after an exploded tyre had seriously damaged his hand. He is an emotional man who empathizes with the sadness of others. He is also an impulsive man who instantly offers help. Above all, he is a practical man who ensures that the help is meaningful.

Such a man is involved with what might loosely be called charitable acts for those he knows. His employees and friends talk frequently of his gentleness and compassion when people have problems. When Charles Gwathmay's mother died, Ricky and Ralph took him and Bette-Ann to Montego Bay to help them recover from the ordeal. It was the sort of help that Ralph Lauren gives: instant, practical, informal and unrecorded.

As further evidence of Ralph and Ricky's personal generosity, the Ralph and Ricky Lauren Center for the Performing Arts at Lexington School for the Deaf was set up in June 2002, funded by a gift of $2 million from the Laurens. The center, a 33 year-old school auditorium, is a modern, fully equipped arts venue, which acknowledges the importance of performance arts for deaf and partially deaf children. It is the fruition of the long association the Laurens have had with the Lexington School, since they were introduced to its work by one of Ralph's lifelong friends from his Bronx days, whose parents were deaf. Ralph Lauren's involvement with charity is the positive response of a practical man of who Edgar Bronfman says, "He looks around corners to discover his own realities."

living the dream

Film, the most powerful medium of the twentieth century, might well be seen by future generations as the only valid manifestation of modern culture in the past hundred years, with poetry, song, and literature being considered, as easel painting already is, nothing more than atavistic clinging to an intellectual ideal both discredited and exhausted. If it were to happen, then Ralph Lauren's attitude to life, behavior, dress, and environment will be seen to have been remarkably forward-looking. It is possible to see the world he has created as a worldwide Universal Studio lot. Whether we buy into his particular dream or not we all live our lives to a certain degree as if we were acting in a drama.

Television has made even the least imaginative of us self-regarding, rather as if we were viewing ourselves as performers on a screen. It can also be claimed that our homes are similarly, and largely subconsciously, arranged, lit, and accessorized with the same end in view. The dramatic twentieth-century advances in democracy, technology, and prosperity gave a high proportion of the population of the Western world, at least, the opportunity to live life as it had previously only been enjoyed by the wealthy and privileged. We could change our clothes—our whole appearances, if we wished—with a prodigality which had earlier been entirely the province of the rich. We could pamper ourselves with cures, beauty products, and health spas in a way in which no previous civilization had been able. Even more, we could decorate our homes to achieve comfort, ease, and luxury, rather than the purely practical considerations of previous centuries.

Ralph and Ricky Lauren were brought up in modest circumstances, but there was a spirit in their family homes which had to do with more important things than wealth. Love, warmth, contentment, and common beliefs are what make a home. In Ralph's case another element also lifted his life out of the post-Depression, wartime America in which he was brought up: the artistic flair of his father, who played his violin to conjure up and perhaps quieten memories of the past and, above all, painted simple bucolic scenes to hang on the walls of the family's small apartment. It is not difficult to visualize the young Ralph gazing at those pictures, more colorful and vital than the furnishings around which he had crawled or the view from the window to which his parents lifted him up in order to look out. Both framed picture and window can be seen as precursors for the film screen which was soon to come into his life.

Ralph Lauren's later dreams in the perfect homes he saw in the movies of the forties and fifties. For such a visually sensitive boy these films opened up vistas of perfection, sophistication, and elegance, offering surroundings where life could only be gracious and good. Ricky Lauren recalls how in their very first house as a newly married couple with little money, they decorated the walls with pictures clipped from magazines. They converted utilitarian spaces like the kitchen area and bathroom into visual seminars where their eyes and their tastes were trained by the photographs from *Vogue* and *House & Garden*.

The eyes are the secret of Ralph Lauren's success. In the early years he moved forward from the visual approach of his teenage years, which was purely cinematic, to develop a point of view more photographic. One of the reasons for his huge success as a retailer is that he presents his vision in terms most Americans can understand: the frozen moment of the still photograph, capturing a split second of perfection, an instant of happiness which makes even the casual viewer flicking nonchalantly through a magazine pause and wish to be part of that world.

When it came to organizing the visuals of his personal, private world, that photographic eye ensured that, in the several apartments in which he and Ricky lived for the first few years of their marriage, nothing was ever visually random. Even when they could afford to buy only one small object per month to enhance their homes, it was never a casual purchase. How could it be in a man who takes counsel on all things and mulls over every decision, seeing it from every possible angle, before making the final choice? He was lucky in that his wife, who shared his eagerness to train the eye, understood his visual perceptions and brought her own knowledge of art and literature to the equation.

What Ralph lacked in broad cultural terms Ricky was frequently able to supply, but both admit that in their first married years in the sixties, they were on a learning curve of taste. It was exhilarating and challenging and it meant endless trips to Barneys, Bloomingdale's, and the little design shops that were springing up, often specializing in imported goods such as the highly popular plates designed by the Italian Piero Fornasetti, which enjoyed worldwide popularity with people wishing to appear modern, design-conscious, and artistic. Ralph and Ricky were part of a vast young crowd of newly marrieds, soon-to-be-weds, or going-steadies who dreamed Saturday afternoons away in the stores, building a hundred different lifestyles and spinning enchanted worlds of perfect happiness before buying a hamburger and then a different sort of dream in a Third Avenue movie house.

Even then Ralph Lauren was able to look a little wider and imaginatively encompass a little more than other young dreamers. He and his new wife had little money to spare but limited

Above left and right: One of Ralph and
Ricky's first apartments in New York.

"Even if we still thought a particular look was beautiful, we knew it was time to make another look—in a different apartment."

Right: Perfection for the visual connoisseur.

budgets do not necessarily lead to impoverishment of spirit. Even the most depressing of days spent attempting to sell ties to guys who were too frightened to try to understand, too stuck in their safe and comfy little cocoons to dare to be open to any suggestion of the new—and there were many such days—could not dim Ralph's burning vision. That vision encompassed how he and his family should live just as much as it encompassed how, through his efforts, they would be able to live to the standard of grace and eclecticism that was becoming increasingly important to him. In the words of one of the most popular numbers in *The Pajama Game*, Richard Adler and Jerry Ross's endlessly optimistic musical which opened in New York in 1954 and ran for over a thousand performances: "Two cents doesn't buy a helluva lot / but only ten years from today / that's enough to buy / a foreign car / only twenty years today / I'll buy myself a pajama factory / and have them work for me." They were sentiments Ralph could totally understand.

Geraldine Stutz, one of several key figures in Ralph's early days who understood his sensibility and admired his singlemindedness, recalls how his antennae led him to a quixotic little shop on the Upper East Side called San Francisco, between Seventieth and Seventy-First on the east side of the street, where it remains today. "There was never anything of enormous import there," she admits. "But the marketing approach was something Ralph admired. It wasn't just the merchandise, it was the presentation—a fustier, mustier, dustier approach to the one Ralph finally settled on for his shops but in the same spirit. It was one of a number of little shops of that kind and it had a cult following." It was that sense of presentation that fitted Ralph's need for visual activity and busyness in the many visual mise-en-scènes he was to create in both his shops and his homes.

Writing of a man so emotionally involved with movies, it is irresistible to take his obsession a little further and see him as a multifaceted version of the great Hollywood stock characters: the head of studio, the producer, the director and the star; the man who gets to make all the decisions. Not even Daryl F. Zanuk controlled his studio more completely and efficiently. David O. Selznick never had budgets to compare with those with which Ralph has worked to create—and maintain—the dream environment of his five homes. Could Otto Preminger outbid him in his demands for special effects, or Cary Grant and Katharine Hepburn even hope for more diverse roles than those played by Ralph and Ricky? Together, they choose the setting, decide on the clothes, work out the steps, and virtually script the life they decide to "film" at any of their paradise retreats.

Each of Ralph Lauren's homes is as perfect of its type as money, time, and painstaking attention to detail can ensure. Regardless of whether each appeals to individual tastes, what they have in common is a level of quality which, within its generic type, is perfectly judged. Further, they are refined, visually sophisticated, and clearly conceived to reflect, but not advertise, a point of view. These are houses, not showcases; the Laurens guard their privacy very closely, rarely allowing in journalists and cameramen (on average once every ten years or so) and inviting as guests only family members, highly trusted and valued employees, business associates and friends: a *corps d'élite* stretching over years.

Ralph Lauren is not a privileged aristocrat, cut off from the world. He is a hard-working design entrepreneur who meets in his daily business many people from within and without his

organization—hundreds per week. There is nothing ivory tower about his world, any more than there is with Ricky's. As a therapist and counsellor, she is even closer to the wellspring of humanity. But unlike many people under pressure, the Laurens distance themselves in the true eighteenth-century patrician manner on an almost weekly basis. This is when they use their homes in order to breathe again air of a purity long denied New Yorkers. For the Laurens, their homes are their lungs: emotionally, spiritually, and physically. It is a rare weekend when Ralph and Ricky, very often with their children, are not leaving Manhattan by helicopter for the airport or driving north to upstate New York. Occasionally Ralph takes a long weekend, leaving on Thursday afternoon and returning before Monday evening if he is traveling from Jamaica. If he is going to the Montauk beach house or the estate at Bedford, Westchester, the time might be less and trips to the ranch in Telluride, Colorado, are normally confined to longer vacation periods, always during the summer months. In each one the Laurens find their own carefully constructed and perfectly kept cinematic paradise gardens.

It was not like this when Ralph began his career. There was little money to spend on the home but dreamers do not live too much in the present. "He's very romantic," Ricky Lauren says of her husband. "When I met him, I was nineteen. He took me into his dream world—which was not so different from the dream world that was half-forming in my mind, because my parents prepared me for it by bringing me up in a very European style. We were—even at the beginning—on the same wavelength because he wanted that style and glamor."

When they first married, the vision was indeed purely a dream. The reality for Ralph was long hard days as a tie salesman, for Ricky equally demanding work as a teacher. Ricky recalls, "I knew all the tricks and when the children came along I juggled them, the cooking, and the housework." She remembers their first home, which they set up in 1964 in the Bronx, as a place of great happiness. "There was a sunken living room and casement windows. My father-in-law was so sweet. He knew I wanted a rich European wood feel to the room and he would come over and work into the late hours to create a marvelous rich brown panelled mahogany effect. It was fabulous. We were so proud and excited. Then we had to decorate around it."

Like other young marrieds, the Laurens used ingenuity to circumvent their lack of funds. They went out of their way to find unusual things in thrift shops. A Bohemian impulse led them to seek out beautiful old rugs that they could throw over furniture, to match the brown velvet throw on a sleeping sofa which, Ricky recalls, had imitation furs on top. "We loved it and were so excited," she laughs. "There were two steps and railings down to the sunken living room and I remember us painting them gold, staying up until two in the morning to finish. We painted the casement windows a bronzy gold color to go with the faux mahogany. It was our own castle!" Ralph's father was equally enthused and would bring them treasures he had found, such as an armchair which, Ricky remembers, "was a Louis-type piece of furniture, like a mini throne. He painted it beautifully and I re-covered it. We had very eclectic taste and we mixed it with rattan and wrought-iron chairs. It worked, as well. We had a folding metal card table and some director's chairs so we could entertain friends, although we didn't have a proper kitchen. We had what was called a Pullman kitchen, which was very simple, but I could make wiener schnitzel and things like that. Otherwise we'd eat out after seeing a movie."

She especially remembers the bedroom. "It had light-blue walls and floral curtains and bedspread, in aqua and green. We had a Princess telephone next to the bed, quite different from the one in the living area. We thought it was very special because it was blue and it was quite something to have a blue telephone when everybody was used to a black rotary dial. We were very advanced for our time. We didn't bother with a bed. We just had a mattress on the floor. Then my sister-in-law's parents got us a box spring mattress and metal frame. We were very excited."

These were the beginnings. In the first years of their marriage, they moved several times, on each occasion to a slightly better locale or a more generously proportioned property, as they slowly climbed the ladder, such as Seventy-Fourth Street in Manhattan, their second home, with an L-shaped living–dining room and a kitchen—with a window which, as Ricky recalls, "was quite a big deal for New York." Each time, in her words, their taste became more refined: an inlaid French commode "with a creamy marble top," custom-made chairs covered in needlepoint, and even a hand-painted chandelier in turquoise and gold, with white flowers. It was in those early days that their love affair with denim and navy blue for upholstery and coverings began—it has never left them. Even today, their poolside chairs are covered in Ralph Lauren trademark navy, and denim has long been a staple part of the merchandise in the Polo Ralph Lauren home range.

Although there was some consistency as they developed their mutual design eye, the Laurens were always receptive to the newest ideas in interiors magazines or at antique fairs and home-decorating promotions in the major New York stores. "We always knew when it was time to change," Ricky claims. "Even if we still thought a particular look was beautiful, we knew it was time to make another look—in a different apartment. But some things were always consistent. Our bedroom was kept simple and the color that we used to carry through the whole apartment was almost always blue, or white. We gradually had a little more money to spend but we always had to use our ingenuity—which was typical of a lot of young people in the city at that time."

Like all lives run on a budget, the not very important things often became very big matters, remembered long after the event. Ricky recalls their first color television: "That was a big deal for us. It must have been around Christmas because I remember them installing it late—you know how they work late just before Christmas—and we couldn't believe it. We stayed up almost all night watching it. Young kids now have no idea of that sort of excitement because they see it practically the very first time they open their eyes," but for the Laurens it was an eye-opener, as it would be for people for whom color is so vitally important. But what really inspired them were magazines. "We were always flagging pages—not for an item to buy but for a look which we found interesting, something that we could adapt and personalize to make it work for us. Our favorite store for ideas was Sloanes, near Lord & Taylor. It was always full of young couples, browsing. It was very intense. Nobody talked. It was as if they were in a museum."

All three of the Lauren children were born within two-and-a-half years of each other, in Mount Sinai hospital which, Ricky recalls, was rather like an extended family crèche. "Everybody knew us there," she says. "My sister-in-law had her three children there and we had our three there as well. So, with Jerry's family and ours there were six children born in the same hospital on the same floor with the same nurses. Andrew was born on May 7, 1969. David was October 31, 1971. It was Halloween—a holiday I've always loved. I remember us trying to get out of the building on Seventy-Fourth Street to get me to the hospital and, of course, everyone was trick-or-treating. I

Overleaf left: Ralph and Ricky in East Hampton, 1976.
Overleaf right: Ralph with his three children in East Hampton, 1977.

was having labor pains and all the buttons on the elevator had been pressed so that we stopped at every single floor. Things were calmer for Dylan. She was born on May 9, 1974. And then the family parading in to visit. Everybody knew my parents, the in-laws, and the brothers and sisters."

As the family coffers grew, so did the dimensions of the homes. Shortly after David's birth, the Laurens found their first real apartment. It had a small terrace around which they put a wooden picket fence. As Ricky remembers, "In New York, needless to say, white wood doesn't stay that way for five minutes! We painted it ourselves and we put trees in tubs out there and we had a green-and-white striped awning, like the beach chairs you can rent in England." They also had white sofas, something again they were to keep as part of their decorating vocabulary for life, along with leather chairs and glass tables. "I remember we had a sliding mirror-glass door for one wall, behind which we had closet space—which is always a big issue in New York. We also had the same mirror treatment for the kitchen door, so that when you walked into the apartment you didn't know it was a kitchen door. It was all quite eclectic—fabric painting from India, which I still have; blue-and-white *jardinières*; one of those blue-and-white ceramic elephants, with the glass top you can just about put a glass on and that's all. Very typical of young couples' apartments at the time." And there were rugs everywhere. Antique Persian ones: "They had to be exactly the right ones. The dimensions had to be exactly so. We were into reds and blues and the darker colors by then. I remember in the den we had a denim couch that was a sleep sofa, which we put with a rattan-and-bamboo chair and a dark mahogany desk. And we had louvred shutters made for the windows. It was very dark and elegant—and a little mysterious. In contrast, the whole dining room was mirrored."

Ricky Lauren has always seen her role as being pre-eminently that of homemaker for her husband and their children. Always involved in decorating their homes, she is a practical person who clearly could have made a good living as an interior decorator. "I would talk to the construction people who came to work on our apartments," she says, "to learn the physics of things. I was always good at that. I enjoy making things work." She remembers when Ralph was on a business trip to Europe and she was pregnant with Dylan: "I went to town and had a lot of fun putting in my own touches. When David and Andrew were asleep, I was on ladders climbing all over their room. I always did things to occupy my time when Ralph had to go away. I hated it when he traveled. I'd wallpaper the kitchen, make louvre doors using a drill gun, then I'd paint and hang them myself. In the apartment we had before our present one, I wallpapered the children's room in red-and-white gingham check and I made a molding out of navy-and-white adhesive tape around the ceiling. I used to do needlepoints of cars for the children and fox-hunting scenes for us. But then we moved to our present apartment, which is so much bigger, and we had the help of a professional interior decorator with it."

If Ralph and Ricky shared a passion for their home and how it looked, Ricky was on her own in the kitchen. "Ralph never cooked," she says firmly. "I did all the cooking—which I love." She acknowledges that their eating habits have changed since the early days of their marriage. Now the emphasis is on healthy food, whereas when they were younger they ate a lot of red meat. "Ralph's favorite is lamb chops," she says. "Or the organic steaks from our ranch. We've always eaten chicken and when we were first married I usually did a fish dish once a week but he never really liked fish in those days. Now we eat fish a lot, but then it would be rib steaks, schnitzel, and liver. And Ralph is like all Americans: nobody can pass up a great hamburger!"

Some of the happiest memories for Ralph, Ricky, and their family were of the vacations they took with the children. For some time they rented a shingle house in East Hampton with a white picket fence where they took the children at weekends and for vacations. It was the sort of simple, healthy, uncomplicated outdoor life to which the family responded. Their lives on Long Island with their young children were spent almost entirely out of doors, cycling, walking, playing ping-pong (one of Ralph's favorite games) and basketball. It is a pattern which has been maintained in their family vacations—even now.

The house in the Hamptons was rented on a yearly basis so that they could go whenever they wished—an arrangement that lasted for eleven years until they found the perfect beach house right at the end of Long Island, in Montauk, adjacent to the Hamptons, which over the years had become increasingly chi-chi and fashionable. The house at Montauk had been designed by an American architect, trained under Frank Lloyd Wright and in Japan, and was a simple, small, but memorable structure perfectly sited within the landscape, hidden from the road and with uninterrupted ocean views. It had not been a family home for some years, having been used as a vacation let. Initially, the Laurens rented also, but they soon decided that they wanted it to be a permanent vacation base, so they bought it.

The main house has a Zen-like quality of calm that the Laurens have preserved. Its simplicity and purity need no improving. But, as a small building, designed to be a compact family vacation home, Ralph and Ricky felt that it needed to be augmented by other buildings. Rather than spoil the integrity of the existing house by adding wings to it, they decided on a pattern they would use in other homes in the future. The main house would be the center of a core with other, satellite buildings radiating from it. They bought the neighboring property, which gave them about seven acres to landscape, with buildings as an integral part of the design. Taking existing structures—the stable, a garage—they built a guesthouse, a screening room, and, a little way from the pool, a gymnasium, all in the local vernacular of rough stone and wood with shingle roofs—and all so skilfully placed in their setting and surrounded by clever planting that they look not only entirely indigenous but also so established that they could be imagined to have been on the site for at least a hundred years. Most are covered with climbing plants, predominantly ivy.

The whole estate is sheltered from the public gaze, although the long, straight beach that runs below the slight bluff on which the house rests is a public one, where people walk dogs and families have picnics. Normally, meals are taken in the grounds, at sites that give uninterrupted ocean vistas but provide privacy from the beach below. It would be possible to walk the beach many times before even realizing that there was a property above it. Nothing but a small, white-painted gate in the dunes gives any hint of habitation. Climbing up the scrubby slope, one discovers an English-style lawned terrace with a dining table and chairs at its far end. It is one of several places where the family can eat. There is a terrace dining area immediately outside the living room of the main house and one near the pool. The last is the family's favorite place for lunch, under the shade of the lichen-covered trees and only a few steps from the pool or the jacuzzi. The pool, protected by Scots pines and rhododendrons, is much more subtle than most American pools with their garish technicolor turquoise.

Below the pool is a tennis court, which is the focus of attraction for the children, brought up not only to be active but also highly competitive in the sports arena. Ralph Lauren looks back to his own childhood and is convinced that the right attitude to sport is an essential part of

Their lives on Long Island with their young children were spent almost entirely out of doors, cycling, walking playing ping-pong (one of Ralph's favorite games) and basketball.

A relaxed father spending time with his
children in East Hampton, 1976.

character-forming in children. Even when the children were young, he and Ricky taught them the importance of being wholehearted in their competitions and, in Ricky's words, to be "generous to each other in victory or defeat." Ralph says, "In sport as in life, the only person you are competing against is yourself. The other guy—or the other team—is only there to help you get the best out of yourself." But it helps to have the right equipment and the gym at Montauk is full of state-of-the-art body-building and exercise machinery. Ralph and Ricky, often with their own personal trainers who come out from New York, spend many hours of their Montauk day working out there.

As with the Lauren houses in Jamaica and Colorado, this is an outward-looking place, where fresh air is the driving force. Again, as with the other properties, the views from the windows have been carefully orchestrated so that each one—whether a panorama or a fleeting glimpse—is perfect. All encompass the garden, landscaped by Randolph Marshall, the man who has redesigned the grounds of all Ralph's homes, and kept perfect by three gardeners who come in on a weekly basis.

The buildings are mainly wood-lined, including ceilings, all being stained a golden tan color that reflects the sun and contrasts with the predominantly white-covered soft furnishings—long comfortable sofas and deep armchairs. Much of the furniture is bamboo, made especially in Bali, and the overall feeling is reminiscent of the Lauren safari style of the eighties. In keeping with the simplicity, the only pictures are photographs, many of them black and white and several taken by Ricky Lauren on her safari to Kenya and her trip to China. The mood is deliberately low-key and simple. If there is a Zen feeling to the buildings, the living room in the main house, with its long wooden mantel above a stone fireplace, also has the organic quality found in many of the houses designed by Frank Lloyd Wright.

In scale and mood, Montauk contrasts sharply with the Lauren's other home within easy distance of New York, their 250-acre country estate in Bedford, Westchester County, built by the architectural firm of Delano and Aldrich in 1919—with a long look at the traditions of Europe. It is reminiscent of several building types: French or Belgian châteaux, Scottish castles, and, pre-eminently, the smaller type of manor house still found in its hundreds scattered across the English shires. The mood is summed up in one of Ralph Lauren's advertisements from the mid-eighties: "There is a way of living that has a certain grace and beauty … an appreciation of what has come before … a depth and quality of experience that is lived and felt … this is the quality of life that I believe in."

Ralph and Ricky Lauren saw the essence of Bedford but had to put in a great deal of thought to make it a reality—their reality. In fact, it initially did not seem to have what they required, at all. Mike Farina, an old friend of Ralph's who was an illustrator for the menswear newspaper *Daily News Record*, a colleague of Buffy Birrittella's, and the first man to illustrate a Polo tie, remembers Ralph's misgivings. They hadn't seen each other for some years and then he learned about Ralph's brain tumor. He telephoned Ralph when he had recuperated and they agreed to meet at another Lauren landholding at Pound Ridge, also in Westchester. Farina was involved in real estate at this time, having damaged his hand and being unable to draw, and he and Ralph talked about the Bedford house. At that point, it seemed totally wrong for the Laurens. It had

Everything in the landscape was measured against one of the world's shrewdest and most distinctive eyes.

the sort of prissy garden features, such as stepping-stones across ponds and pagoda buildings, which Ralph and Ricky loathed. The house had been decorated for a quick sale, with every room painted a different color.

But there was something about Bedford which made them all reluctant to move away from it. They knew that speculative builders wished to turn it into a development and they all felt it was too good for that. Farina negotiated the purchase on Ralph's behalf. In return, Lauren asked his friend to look after the estate. Despite his misgivings, Mike Farina eventually agreed. That was in 1989 and he is still in charge of Bedford, a place he has grown to love as much as the Laurens do, a place in which he is emotionally deeply involved, a place to which he gives endless creative thought, changing and improving while creating the sort of character he knows Ricky and Ralph wish it to have. "We don't want anything pompous," Ralph told him. "It's a home; a family house where we can all be close together and feel cosy, not sit at opposite ends of a room and shout at each other."

From the start, there was no question of building. The house was a manageable size and would remain so. There was a caretaker's cottage already and a house across the road from the estate which Ralph bought to preserve his privacy. The only thing that has been specially built is a pool house. One of the unusual features of the estate is a wood-and-glass house designed by Robert Venturi for the son of the previous owners, now used as a studio by Ricky. The Laurens' main concern has been with the grounds, which were in need of complete re-landscaping. As Farina says, "Everything had been totally neglected and had just gone back to nature. At one time there had been a farm but it had become totally overgrown with tulip trees and vines so it all had to be cleared away. The great problem there were no mature standard trees because we have so many deer up here and they eat everything. Most of the trees were decayed and dying, with bad cavities, and covered in weeds. The original ones planted at the time the house was built were all on their last legs. So we brought in trees. But first we bulldozed acres of land, leveled it, brought in tons of fill and topsoil, and built walks where there were previously rocky outcrops. We restructured fields and meadows."

The positioning of the house did not fit in with Ralph and Ricky's aesthetic when they first bought the property. The wife of the man who built it had suffered from a mild form of agoraphobia, and she did not want the building to be in the middle of an area surrounded by lawns. As a result, the house was positioned toward the back of the property, with a phalanx of woodland behind it. Ralph and Ricky felt that the trees enclosed the house too much so they blasted away rock and pushed the level ground back to create four acres of lawn, using the blasted rock to build a poolhouse and a tennis court.

Attention to detail suffuses every aspect of Bedford. Ann Boyd recalls the role she played in obtaining the right flagstones in France for the stone floors. "There is a core of tungsten in Ralph," she says. "I mean a good core, not an evil one. You know very soon that there will be no point in trying to cut corners because, despite that gentleness—and I could listen to that voice for ever—he never gives up. You always know that you will get it right for him in the end. This is his secret. This is his leadership skill. He is steely in his perfectionism and that is what we all respond to. When we were doing things for Bedford I was very useful to him because I speak French, Italian and German, and many of the things we obtained were found on the continent. For example, I shipped over limestone floors from France, which were painstakingly matched for colour and texture."

Ralph was right to be very precise about the floors. They play a large part in setting the tone of Bedford. As one moves from room to room, the feeling of the place becomes more precise. It is England, with a little touch of France and quite a lot of old Newport glamor: the kitchen with its mahogany cupboards, brass rails, and rows of copper pans; the breakfast room, smelling of old wood smoke, with its antler-horn chandelier and vast old pine dresser piled high with pewter, porcelain, and chipped earthenware platters; the dining room with its richly polished mahogany table, carvers at both ends and eight place settings each side, and a bone-handled carving set with a three-foot-long blade to the knife and huge prongs to the fork on a long Victorian sideboard. The dark-green fabric-covered walls are a perfect foil for the gilt mirrors and the eclectic collection of pictures, including a Landseer drawing of lions, a Victorian woman riding a hunter, black-and-white photographs of cowboys and old racing cars, and crossed antlers above the doors.

The atmosphere of a family home where personal mementos—often of little intrinsic value—are treasured as much as valuable pictures or pieces of furniture grows stronger as one walks through the house, noting a Rayburn portrait; a picture by Joseph Wright of Derby; photographs of Ralph Lauren with the Princess of Wales; a library entirely lined in tartan, with zebra-skin-covered poufs, paintings of lions and tigers, Indian chieftains and warriors masks; family photographs everywhere. Different layers of sensation represent diverse personalities in a complex family mix—the traveler, the scholar, the sportsman, and the connoisseur all have their little vignettes in this decor, which looks as if it has slowly grown over several generations. The house expresses the potency of Lauren's vision. Bedford is a microcosm of the world Lauren offers to us all, not only through his merchandise but also by his finely drawn approach to display. More than anywhere else, with the exception of the Rhinelander mansion, Bedford displays the roots of a major portion of the Lauren vision.

When visiting Double RL, the Lauren ranch in Colorado, it is tempting to speculate as to whether Ralph as a toddler heard on the family radio the Andrews Sisters singing "Don't Fence Me In," their hit song from the 1943 film *Stagedoor*, with its refrain, "Give me land, lots of land, in the country that I love, Don't fence me in." After all, he did once claim, "I love land. I'm a land junkie. I want the freedom. I want to feel the air." And if that makes him sound like a character out of Edna Ferber's novel *Giant*, it must be remembered that he is speaking for millions of his fellow Americans, even though they probably haven't been brought up on the Andrews Sisters' song. What they are all longing for is not simply land, but the most potent land of all for Americans: the West, the home of the American dream and the foundation of the American myth. When Ralph and Ricky Lauren took their children on vacation to Sante Fe in the early eighties it crystallized their thinking to a remarkable degree. As Ricky has said, "We always loved the idea of the West and even as children we wanted to be cowboys and cowgirls. I wanted to be a cowgirl so badly! There's a picture of Ralph as a cowboy when he was a little boy and there's a picture of me as a little girl dressed as a cowgirl. So you can see," she jokes, "we were ready-dressed for it."

After a lot of searching they found what they had been looking for in Colorado, in a tiny settlement a few miles from Telluride, itself 260 miles south west of Denver. They discovered Ridgway through Michael Martin Murphy, a country-and-western singer who had become a friend through his wife Mary, who had been a model for Ralph. A place with a population of 500 within Ouray county, itself home to just 3,000 souls, Ridgway is set in gloriously unspoilt countryside, recognized by the Unites States Forest Service when they classified Highway 62, which

Above: The outdoor life in Colorado.

For two souls enmeshed with the West, the Colorado home has a special resonance for Ralph and Ricky Lauren.

runs through it, as a national scenic by-way. Very conscious of the fragile balance of the beauty of such an area, Ralph Lauren has pointed out, "When I first came out to Colorado, I didn't want to build a new house. I wanted to find an old one. I love the look, the beauty of undisturbed land. Driving by on the road, you could miss the Lodge, our family house." As he frequently points out, this is not just a home but a serious working ranch supporting over a thousand head of crossbreed Black Angus steers, run by cowboys who keep the old skills alive and are as conscious as the Laurens of the vulnerability of land—and their responsibility to it.

In an area of outstanding natural beauty, the Laurens' place manages to be even more beautiful than its surroundings. It consists of high alpine meadows above the treeline, woods of spruce, oak brake, and aspen, cut through by fast-moving creeks with tall cottonwoods on their banks, the whole panorama thrown into relief by the dramatic jagged backdrop of the snow-covered San Juan mountains. Ralph Lauren sums up the effect of this expansive, powerful landscape by saying simply, "I feel so small out here; minute." It is a cliché in a place which attracts clichés, but it is true. This is *Shane* country, where the people are honest but not gullible, simple but not simpletons, where a slow cowboy drawl does not necessarily denote a slow-witted soul. It's a place where city stereotyping slides away to reveal the truths that underlie all myths. The West is a place where the American soul finds peace and comes to terms with itself. It isn't a con, thought up by slick advertising executives; it is a reality, especially for a man like Ralph Lauren, who absolutely believes in what he has described as "the purity of the West."

The oldest building on the ranch, dating from the 1890s and now the guesthouse called the Little Brown Cabin but known to everybody on the ranch as "little brown," was quickly resited when Lauren bought the ranch, being moved about a mile from the main buildings, the cookhouse and the lodge. The result is that it now commands a peerless view of pasture, woodland, and mountains. In a sense it is a paradigm of how the West is changing. If cowboys appreciated natural beauty, it was a side order to a diet of hard work and the endless fight against nature and weather. Cowboys, almost by definition, were intuitive men who rarely had the benefit of an education. Ralph's ranch manager at the time, Larry Luke, could not be further removed from such a stereotype. A former investment adviser from California who quit banking for the open-air life, he runs the Double LR entirely as a business, using all that modern science and technology can offer to improve the quality of the beef the ranch produces. As he explains, "When I came for the job Ralph had already had a manager for two years who didn't work out, and because of that, I asked him for a brief. What he wanted first was to preserve the land in its historical perspective as an operating mountain cattle range. Secondly, to produce the highest possible quality steak. It was that simple."

The ranch is the place where Ricky loves to ride. She learned to do this when she was young. She was keen that her children would have the skill and she feels lucky to have them experience riding out in the West. Ralph has honed his skills under the tutelage of Larry Mahan, six times world-champion bull rider and all-American cowboy, with whom he and Ricky ride. As Larry Luke says, "Ralph enjoys riding cutting horses—the ones used to separate a cow from the herd— and they're very quick." When the family goes to Colorado for their summer break in July, Ralph and Ricky ride every day, fittting it into their training, jogging, and walking fitness schedules, for the sheer joy of seeing their land in the best way possible: from the saddle. They are excited by the teaming wildlife of the area, from elk and mountain lions to brown bears, and are always on the lookout for the sudden encounter, the close-up confrontation which, as Ricky says, makes them feel "proud and humble that [they] are helping preserve the habitat of such potentially vulnerable creatures." Larry tells the story of how once, when Ralph was walking across the meadows, he came face to face with a bear. "He was very cool about it. The bear was less than 30 feet away. Ralph said to me, 'I don't know who was more surprised.'"

This would not be a Ralph Lauren spread if everything were not absolutely perfect. As always, Ralph's team of surrogate eyes and ears was there from the start to intuit and fulfill his needs. The building which the Laurens now refer to as the Lodge was designed by their friend Ted Mayes from ideas put forth by Ralph and Ricky. Naomi Leff and Buffy were called in to add a functionality to the existing structure (i.e. mud room, closets) and Buffy provided the finishing details to turn the Lodge into a home. Buffy took on the West in her quest to add authenticity to Double RL. She knew clearly that only the authentic would interest Ralph. She appreciated his dismay at how quality had begun to disappear from the Western scene.

Ralph had been working with local people whom he had assumed were getting the ranch the way he wanted it. He would talk to them, explain his vision, and discuss specifics. Then he would go back to New York and leave them to do what he'd asked. Far too many times when he returned three or four months later it was to be disappointed. For months when he and Ricky went to the ranch they had had to stay in a trailer without even a closet in which to hang their clothes. He knew that all the bones of a perfect ranch were there but it was not coming together and they were growing disheartened.

As Buffy sees it, the problem was a culture clash between the manager (this was before the time of Larry Luke) and his wife, who were jointly supervising things, and Ralph. The firm had just launched the home collection—it was 1983—and Buffy had supervised the building of a log cabin showroom designed by Naomi Leff for one of the themes of the collection. She had been shooting the collection at Sundance in Utah, had built a log cabin showroom, and had commissioned a local workman to make a log bed for the shoot.

When Ralph walked through the log-cabin display room, Naomi Leff remembers he had tears in his eyes. "It's perfect," he said to her. "This is exactly what I want for my ranch. You guys are doing it for my company and yet I can't get it done for myself. Do it for me." It was not only a commission, it was a challenge. Buffy Birrittella remembers it was February and the deadline for getting everything done was the end of June, ready for the family to go to the ranch for the month of July. "So, it was making the cookhouse work, redoing the little brown cabin and completely doing the Lodge—it didn't even have a mud room. You came directly from outside to the house. They didn't even really have a bathroom. Ralph had wanted a rock shower and they'd built it entirely of rock and it was so cold and gray, like being in a grotto. Nobody wanted to use it. Ralph and Ricky had amassed a fabulous collection of rare native American blankets and weavings which they were having to keep in storage and yet they didn't even have any furniture. So, essentially, what happened was that I was taking Ralph's private jet every Thursday or Friday after work and spending the weekend in the West sorting everything out. It went on for four months."

Her brief was simple: to turn a work in progress into the perfect Western family home. Ricky and Ralph so trusted her judgment that she rarely had to refer back to them before making a decision. "There was always someone to meet ... I had a schedule of meetings with lock guys who

What they are all longing for is not simply land, but the most potent land of all for Americans: the West, the home of the American dream and the foundation of the American myth.

Dogs have always been an integral part
of the Lauren world.

Above: Ralph with one of his favorite toys in the mountains in Colorado.

could reproduce authentic Old West locks and door fittings ... Ralph didn't like the stone of the fireplace in the lodge so I had to find a stonemason to do it all over again ... Naomi had to brief the contractor, the cabinetmaker, the team that was building the kitchen. I remember we had a lot of trouble getting just the right color for the chinking between the logs of the walls. Ralph was on the phone: 'Now don't make it too gray, don't make it too yellow, don't make it too tan, don't make it too white,' and I'm thinking, 'Oh my God.' The extent of my chinking training and experience is virtually nil, apart from the chinking for the Home Collection showroom. And then the color of the logs! I would be with the guy staining the logs to get the perfect honey color and the perfect finish so that it's not too glossy, not too dull, not too gray, not too this, not too that … and I would be, 'Oh, my God, I hope I'm right!' But that's Ralph. He totally empowers you. But then, you know, he trained me to understand all the nuances he wanted."

For the layout of the kitchen Buffy and Naomi worked with Ricky but for the most part Buffy worked directly with local tradespeople. "I would arrive," she recalls, "on Friday night, then take the plane and fly to Santa Fe or Denver to buy things on Saturday morning. Ralph and Ricky had already bought valuable chief's blankets that could hang on the wall or drape a piece of furniture, but you couldn't walk on them. I had to find the functional items (rugs, etc.) to add to their incredible artwork. I was using the plane like a pick-up truck. Every Saturday afternoon we'd be loading the steer heads or whatever! I became very popular in Santa Fe. I wouldn't be in the place for five minutes before the phone was ringing off the wall. She's here! 'Have I got a rug for you….' 'Ralph asked to see this….' 'I know you're going to love this….' So finally we got it all finished."

As unveiling grew closer, Ralph and Ricky flew in and stayed at the trailer until the Lodge was ready. Buffy and her team were still fiendishly hanging pictures and rugs and putting in the finishing touches. It was agreed that they would come out at twilight. Naomi recalls it had been raining all day and as the Laurens drove down to the Lodge a rainbow arched above it. "It was so perfect," Buffy says. "I was crying and so were they. They were just bowled over at what we'd done. Ralph said to me, 'I don't know how to thank you for doing this for us.' And, of course, although it had been fun, it had been exhausting, like having a different job at the weekends. I didn't have to do it. Then he said, 'We're going to get you a Porsche for doing this for us.' Then I really cried. We had to order it. A red one."

For two souls enmeshed with the West, the Colorado home has a special resonance for Ralph and Ricky Lauren. Although they occasionally fly out to it for short breaks, it is essentially a long-break summer vacation home. That is one of the reasons why it is the place where they truly relax, giving themselves time to unwind and regear their lives to a different pace. The Laurens are hosts in the old and rather grand style in which guests are invited to enjoy their home but not to crowd their lifestyle. The Laurens keep an element of privacy, even with those who are close to them, while providing everything a guest could require. The Lodge has bedrooms only for Ralph and the children. As at Montauk, guests stay in satellite buildings, each of which has its own jeep—or two—so that they can move around the ranch when they want; get to and from the cookhouse easily and quickly, or to visit the screening room, where there are films every night. It is one of the most entertaining buildings in any of Ralph's homes. A tongue-in-cheek re-creation of the archetypal Western saloon bar, with a long counter backed by a mirrored bar stocked with bottles and glasses, a footrail, bar stools, a gaming table, and a vast leather sofa in front of the ceiling-high stone fireplace, it has touches of humor, such as the full-sized painting based on Goya's *Naked*

Maja over the bar and, on the counter, a book on prostitutes in the early days of the West, with the title *Soiled Angels*. Through swing doors is the projection room, entirely modern with its remote-control black-out system and window equipment.

There are five guest cottages, placed in the landscape in order to merge with their surroundings. Each one is the dream of the little house on the prairie brought to perfection, with every modern amenity. Authenticity is of great importance to Ralph Lauren, who views the West as living culture rather than a kitsch, Disney-esque theme park. For every building on the ranch, he searched for authentic, original materials. Logs for wooden floorboards were recycled from derelict barns and abandoned homesteader's cabins to be re-used only after careful aesthetic consideration, so that their new role would reflect and echo their original one. Buffy tells the story of how the cookhouse screen door, made of recycled wood and old hinges, was squeaking and someone suggested that it could use some oil. Ralph responded characteristically. "No, leave it." He said. "That's what makes it great." The cottages are totally private. There are sound systems, televisions and videos and fully equipped kitchens. There are strong, reliable beds with layers of pillows and comforters, topped by antique lace and genuine quilted covers. There are comfortable chairs and sofas, throws and rugs and piles of books, mostly about the culture and art of the West and the traditions of native Americans.

Above all, there are the views. Every window in every cottage reveals a perfect rural scene, usually with the mountains as a magnificent backdrop. A triumph of siting, whether looking out from it or looking at it from outside, each cottage has the feeling of inevitability that makes it right for the landscape—a result achieved by treating the terrain as a landscape painter would. Just as an artist takes license to relocate buildings and trees to create his composition, so every Ralph Lauren landscape is composed in order to achieve the balance and rhythm the painter achieves on his canvas. Ralph's artist's eye has total rigor.

The artistic eye cannot accept things not being correctly placed, whether it is an object on a canvas, a building in a landscape, or something so mundane that most of us would find it easy to ignore, if we even noticed at all. Larry recalls when the family and their house guests were having a cook-out in the high country area of the ranch. It was a simple, casual affair. He remembers it set up "like a scene in a Tom Horn western, with a long table with a tablecloth, ladderback chairs—and all against the backdrop of the mountains. It looked fabulous." Everybody waited for Ralph and Ricky who, as they often do on such occasions, arrived on horseback. But this time, once Ralph had dismounted and gone around the group, greeting and shaking hands, Larry could see that he found something not quite right. Suddenly he enlisted everybody and they moved everything to a new point. It was not more than twenty feet away but he smiled and said, "This is it." As Larry says, "He had to have it just right. Nobody resented it. Everybody was laughing, but it's all part of his keen sense of what fits."

Larry and Karen Luke feel that, if it were possible, the Laurens would spend more time in Colorado and Ralph has said that, whenever he is at the ranch, he feels so completely happy that he invariably fantasizes about staying and running the business from there. But he knows that as long as he is part of the business it will remain a fantasy, something which saddens the Lukes. As Larry says, "We love it when they come because we know they renew their sense of purpose in this place. They live an integrated life here. They recharge their batteries. The peace, the serenity, and the beauty help them to keep their perspective. That's why we like to see them come."

Many of the items in the main home are very valuable because they are unique or the best of their kind. That is why, as with other Lauren homes, everything is numbered, photographed and catalogued—another example of the organization that lies behind the apparently random perfection found in all the Lauren homes. Every surface in the house is a mini-museum of artefacts of the West: traditional ironwork; Navaho rugs; hand-carved wooden bowls; cowboy hats and bandanas; old chaps; and, on the landing, a magnificent saddle by the famous saddlemaker William Bolen, all skilfully mixed with Lauren's own merchandise from Ralph Lauren Home. It is part of Ricky's Austrian inheritance that she likes to have everything ordered, logical and logged, so that there are never any nasty shocks or unexpected surprises. All television sets and music systems are the same make and model.

In the opinion of many in the Lauren organization, Jamaica is where the Laurens feel most totally at peace, even more so than at the ranch in Colorado. "I guess I could see myself retiring there, some day," Ralph has said, but it is probably only a dream. Although full retirement seems unlikely, it is easy to see why Jamaica could be the place in which it might happen. The island is a favorite with the Laurens, as it has been with wealthy sun-seekers since the thirties, when Pan Am flying boats used to sweep low and land in a flurry of white spray on Montego Bay, bringing the smart set from Manhattan for a period of sybaritic relaxation tended by a people not yet scarred by the poverty, social problems, or fears which are the lot of many modern Jamaicans.

The two men who made it chic to take vacations in Jamaica were the novelist Ian Fleming, creator of James Bond, who bought an estate called Goldeneye, and the playwright, entertainer, and satirist Noel Coward, who became a sensation in America with his high-camp cabaret performances at Wilbur Smith's Desert Inn in Las Vegas, whose home was called Firefly. There was another man who put Jamaica on the international map. John Pringle, Jamaican-born, chose Montego Bay as the place to open a hotel complex in 1952. He called it Round Hill, an estate of around 100 acres, less than ten miles west of Montego Bay, sweeping down to a curved beach. Pringle divided it into plots which he sold to private investors to erect bungalows built to his own specifications. As he has written, he wanted Round Hill to look as good as Jamaica could. The bungalows, staggered at decent intervals across the hill, and the hotel, which followed the curve of the bay, were typical of the island's indigenous architecture—shingled roofs, shuttered windows, overhanging eaves to cool the veranda and terraces. The grand properties of Round Hill are to be found at the very top of the hill complex. They have more space and privacy than most of the bungalows below. The Lauren home, High Rock, is the most tucked-away of them all. Nestling at the end of a secluded drive, surrounded by dense woodland, the house is upon you before you are aware of it. The drive opens out into a standing area for cars and you walk up into a villa which is essentially European in atmosphere, although created for an American client by an American architect. Visitors suggest that it has that essential element for the Laurens—an indefinable but tangible sense of Englishness. Ralph contradicts them: "The house isn't English, but it is colonial," he says firmly. Certainly it is gracious, no matter what the original mood the American architect Burral Hoffman was trying to capture for his client, the investment banker Clarence Dillon, when he designed the house in 1954. What is equally certain, the visitor is much more likely to think of Somerset Maugham's *Up at the Villa* than Tennessee Williams' *Suddenly Last Summer*

It looks across the bay and out to the horizon, its terraces hanging over the water like the decks of an ocean-going liner.

upon walking into the high-ceilinged, fan-cooled main room, which looks out through the portico, across the lawn and swimming pool, to the ocean beyond. This is the world of Norman Douglas, not William Faulkner, a world where wealth and passions are lightly worn.

Its position and its protection even from the exclusive world of Round Hill make High Rock Villa something apart. It is possible to stay there for quite long periods and never cast an eye on anyone other than the staff or those invited into the family circle. And this is why it is such an important place for the Lauren family. Its peace and tranquility are not absolute—traffic on the road to the side of the property can be intrusive at times, but as a place to recharge, slow down, and learn to relax again it is the perfect getaway destination. It has the things that Ralph and Ricky need to counteract the rigors of a New York winter. Ralph describes it as "the miracle of summer" and explains its appeal by reference to his younger days. "I've always been a summer sort of guy," he says. "Because I lived for sport when I was a kid, I couldn't wait for the good weather again so that I could go out and play ball or swim. We used to play stick ball until late in the evening— until the sun went down. And this is the luxury of Jamaica for me. It breaks up the winter. We can leave New York in rain or snow, or with temperatures way below zero, and arrive here and it's summer. It means we can step out of time. Instead of waiting six months for summer to come, we can have it in just four hours. And everything is so lush it's like being in the Garden of Eden—air so warm and light you're bathing in it."

The Laurens had discovered the joys of Jamaica before they decided to buy property there. Tony Cunningham, who has looked after the villa for the past eighteen years, remembers them as guests at Round Hill when he worked as a waiter at the hotel. "They came for two visits before they purchased," he recalls. "Quite close together. They came for Christmas 1978 and then the following Easter." Ralph was by then toying with the idea of looking for property, although Ricky was not entirely sure that they needed another home. All the family loved the island, everybody was happy with Round Hill. When that happens with Ralph and Ricky, when they are convinced that they have found a place that speaks to them and answers their needs, that's when their deep-rooted need to make their own nest comes to the fore and they begin to start looking in earnest. Finding the right property is never easy for people like the Laurens. Their fastidiousness demands that they take on nothing second class, and their wealth means they never have to compromise. But adding a new house to a series is one thing—anybody with money can do that—finding a place which can be turned into a home, offering something different from other houses, is a much more serious undertaking. It is something into which the Laurens did not enter casually or quickly in Jamaica, any more than in their other homes.

They looked. They found a place they felt would do. They returned to New York. They lost it. When the Dillon property came up for sale, Ralph did not hesitate. Even though, as he says, "it was dark and a bit run down—Clarence Dillon was quite an old man by then—it was what we wanted: a beautifully shaped, well-proportioned house in a perfect position on an island with the perfect winter climate. We knew there was a lot of work required but its potential was very clear to us."

One of the first things they did was dynamite the area immediately below the portico to make a swimming pool. Then they thinned out some trees and planted others. After that, they took out interior designer Angelo Doughia, interior design consultant for their minimalist apartment overlooking Central Park, and told him what they wanted the house to be. He jumped at the challenge of restoring, reinventing, and re-creating the sort of property the house might have been

Overleaf: The exterior of Round Hill, Jamaica.

Ricky's photographs from Round Hill,
Jamaica.

The Laurens have built there own private paradise and they know it can only remain that way if private perfections are an integral part.

in Jamaica's great days as an outpost for those who liked things run in the English way: Noel Coward and Graham Greene, Grace Kelly and Oscar Hammerstein, Evelyn Waugh and Princess Margaret. Doughia agreed with the Laurens that the mood of the house must not be threatened, so the process of creating the atmosphere his clients required was a careful, tactful one, with every decision considered and reconsidered before changes were agreed.

It was essential to give the house the light and airy feel that it had largely lacked under the previous owner. It was equally essential to temper or deflect the frequently harsh light of the Caribbean. Doughia solved the problem by basing his scheme on the contrast between white walls and furniture and mahogany, Ralph's favorite wood. Stripped mahogany shutters in the living room, along with mahogany architraves for the doors, specially designed sconces for lights, an eighteenth-century roccoco gilt mirror and a marble fireplace, dark-stained floors with sisal rugs laid over them, two Venetian glass-pier mirrors either side of the door with eighteenth-century tables below—all contrasted with modern bamboo and a white-covered seating area in the center of the room surrounding a low glass table to give the archetypal Lauren mix of historicism, modernity, and, above all, comfort. Bedroom in bamboo and white, state-of-the-art bathrooms, a kitchen equipped to professional catering level: the formula gradually took shape.

The patio-portico follows the feeling of relaxed opulence, with generously sprung, deeply padded seating in white, a tiny family bar, and low tables for drinks. But the space is dominated by the dining table, one of several at High Rock strategically placed to catch or avoid the sun as it moves over the property throughout the day. The patio table commands a view across the swimming pool, past the bamboo and banana trees to a classic white wooden garden seat at the end of the lawn. At night the trees, which encircle the house and garden like a protective hand, are lit according to a carefully planned scheme.

The Laurens bought, a Round Hill bungalow originally built for William S. Paley and his socialite wife Babe, for their beach house. At the furthest point of the hotel wing, it is, for all its proximity to the hotel rooms, entirely private and self-contained. It looks across the bay and out to the horizon, its terraces hanging over the water like the decks of an ocean-going liner. The thump of the waves in the rocks below and the surface ripples as the breeze clips the sea are the only discernible sounds and movement.

It is a white cube open on two sides, with guest rooms, bedrooms, kitchen, and bathroom on either side. In this, it involuntarily echoes the plan of High Rock Villa—although this is the only similarity. Under its shingle roof—steep, like that of a French château, in order to deflect the winter rains and winds that can reach hurricane force—the house is extremely simple. The marble floor is white. The roof supports, slats, and underside of the shingles, which include the ceilings for the rooms, are also white. In the summer the shutters are pulled back from the wide windows so that the ocean—violent blue against the white—is seen from every room and the breeze wings through the house unfettered. The mood is sophisticated marine. Teak, brass, glass and white combine with the blue of the cushions and the blue-and-white pottery which, apart from the tropical ferns, are virtually all the color allowed in this all-white environment.

It is little wonder that High Rock holds such a special place in the lives of all the Laurens. For Ralph, it is probably the location in which he finds it easiest, and quickest, to relax. That is why he normally flies there at the end of his fashion show. He and Ricky hate not to go on that day, no matter how late they might arrive. Montego Bay airport stays open late and flights are accepted up

Right: White light and the blue ocean: the holiday dream made reality in the Lauren cottage in Jamaica.

Right: A calm and tranquil place in Lauren paradise.

to 1.00 a.m., Tony meets them with the car, and they can be home an hour later. They never go straight to bed, no matter how exhausted Ralph may feel. They walk out onto the patio, look across the pool to the velvet blue sky, and breathe in the perfume of the night, scented jasmine carried on the breeze. For Ricky, even at night, the air seems to have a texture to it. She feels it caresses the face "like cotton." It is the perfect winding-down half hour and, no matter what the problems left behind in New York, neither of them has difficulty sleeping that night.

chronology

1960s

1967 Ralph Lauren introduces the wide tie, under the label Polo.

1968 Ralph Lauren broadens Polo to include a menswear range.

1969 Polo by Ralph Lauren, the first shop-within-a-shop for menswear, opens in Bloomingdale's, New York City.

1970s

1970 Ralph Lauren wins Coty Award for Menswear.

1971 Ralph Lauren establishes women's range, with a line of tailored shirts for women, based on the cut of men's shirts, sold in Lauren's women's shop-within-a-shop in Bloomingdale's. Introduction of Polo player logo. First Polo store opens in Beverly Hills.

1972 Polo shirt for men introduced in 24 colors, carrying the polo player emblem, and advertised with the slogan: "Every team has its color —Polo has 24." Polo's first women's fashion show.

1974 Ralph Lauren provides men's clothes for the Jack Clayton movie, *The Great Gatsby*, starring Robert Redford and Mia Farrow, all of which come from the current Polo line, with the exception of one pink suit, which was especially designed by Ralph Lauren for the film.

1975 Ralph Lauren receives The American Fashion Award.

1976 Ralph Lauren receives Coty Award for Womenswear and Coty Hall of Fame Award for Menswear.

1977 Ralph Lauren receives Coty Hall of Fame Award for Womenswear. Ralph Lauren provides the clothes for Woody Allen and Mia Farrow in Allen's movie *Annie Hall*, starting a trend for eclecticism with men's and women's clothing used in a classic trendy, vintage mix decided by the individual wearer.

1978 Ralph Lauren launches Westernwear for men and women, based on authentic Western look. Hailed as the man who 'recapture'

America for America' it rebuffs the erroneous impression that Ralph Lauren's fashion is too British.
First fragrances introduced: Lauren and Polo for Men are launched simultaneously, the first time that men's and women's fragrances have been launched together.
Launch of Polo Boyswear.

1979 Pioneering advertising campaigns: 20-page color spreads in magazines, with little or no text, frequently using non-models, in which the clothes are seen as part of an over-all lifestyle. The results, almost cinematic in breadth, captured the public imagination and have been frequently copied.

1980s

1980 New York Times architecture critic, Paul Goldberger claims Ralph Lauren as the true symbol of America in the eighties, over and above iconic figures such as Philip Johnson or Robert Stern.

1981 The Santa Fe collection, based on traditional Navajo Indian colors and decoration and the dress of the Southwest, launches a major fashion look which sweeps the world.
With the opening of the Polo store in London's Bond Street, Ralph Lauren becomes the first American designer to have his own boutique in Europe, in addition to 28 other retail stores internationally.

1982 Ralph Lauren launches home collection – the first designer to create an entire collection of home products.

1985 Ralph Lauren begins his association, which still continues, with the Telluride Film Festival.

1986 Ralph Lauren opens flagship store in the former Rhinelander mansion on Madison Avenue at 72nd street.
Opening of Polo store in Paris.

1989 Ralph Lauren co-founds, with Katharine Graham of The Washington Post, the Nina Hyde Center for Breast Cancer Research at Georgetown University.

1990s

1990 Launch of Safari Ralph Lauren, which wins the Fi Fi Fragrance Star of the Year. It is the first fragrance with a range of products, accessories and home furnishings to complement it.

1991 The first Super Sale, an annual designer sale held in Washington D.C., is sponsored by Ralph Lauren, Vogue and The Washington Post, to raise funds for the Nina Hyde Center. The event continues until 1998 and raises over $3.5 million for research.

1992 Ralph Lauren presented with the Council of Fashion Designers of America Lifetime Achievement Award.
Safari for Men fragrance receives Fi Fi Fragrance Star of the Year.

1993 Ralph Lauren opens his first Polo Sport Store at 888 Madison, opposite the Rhinelander store.
Polo Sport appointed official outfitter to the American team for the America's Cup.

1994 Together with the CFDA, Ralph Lauren founds Fashion Targets Breast Cancer, a campaign that, by 2002, has a global commitment with campaigns in Argentina, Australia, Brazil, Ireland and the United Kingdom.
Ralph Lauren introduces Purple Label, an exclusive range of men's tailored clothing, appearing personally in the first advertising campaign.

1996 Ralph Lauren introduces Polo Sport line for women.
Ralph Lauren and Polo Sport, the Fitness Fragrance, sponsor Polo Sport Race to Deliver, raising money for the charitable organization God's Love We Deliver, to provide hot meals for housebound people with AIDS/HIV.
Ralph Lauren introduces Polo Sport Woman and wins Fi Fi Award for Best National Advertising Campaign.
Polo Ralph Lauren is title sponsor of the Columbia University Film Festival. The sponsorship would continue until 2000.
Polo Jeans Co.——a line of casualwear for the young is launched.
Ralph Lauren receives an Honorary Doctorate of Letters from Brandels University for his commitment to arts and education, and his support for breast cancer campaigns.

Ralph Lauren receives the first Humanitarian Award from the Nina Hyde Center for Breast Cancer, presented by Diana, Princess of Wales.

1997 Ralph Lauren receives CFDA 1996 Menswear Designer of the Year Award.
Polo Ralph Lauren becomes a publicly traded company on the New York Stock Exchange (June 12).

1998 Ralph Lauren fragrance, Romance, is launched. Awarded Fi Fi Fragrance Star of the Year and Fi Fi for best National Advertising Campaign.
Ralph Lauren announces corporate gift of $13 million for the Save America's Treasures Campaign to preserve the Star Spangled Banner.
Polo Sport launches RLX range, authentic high-tech sports clothing. Polo Sport RLX sponsors U.S. World Cup mountain bike team.

1999 Ralph Lauren Fragrance, Romance for Men, is launched and wins Fi Fi Fragrance Star of the Year and Fi Fi for Best National Advertising Campaign.
Ralph Lauren Restaurant opens adjacent to Chicago flagship store, currently the largest Polo store in the world.
Ralph by Ralph Lauren, a collection for 16——25 year old women introduced.
Polo Ralph Lauren acquires Club Monaco.

2000s

2000 Polo.com launched by Ralph Lauren Media.
Voluntary program to build connections between Polo Ralph Lauren employees and their local communities.
Ralph Lauren donates $6 million to set of The Ralph Lauren Center for Cancer Care and Prevention at North General Hospital, Harlem.
Polo Ralph Lauren launches the Pink Pony campaign, to raise awareness of the need for cancer care, using the Polo logo emblem.

2001 Ralph Lauren is inducted into the first Fashion Walk of Fame.
Ralph Lauren fragrance, Glamorous, launched with an advertising campaign featuring Penelope Cruz.

2002 Ralph Lauren sets up The American Heroes Fund in the wake of the World Trade Center attack on September 11th 2001.

acknowledgments

First published in 2002 by
Cassell Illustrated
Octopus Publishing Group Limited
2–4 Heron Quays, London E14 4JP
This paperback edition pubublished in 2005 by Cassell Illustrated
Text copyright © Colin McDowell
Design copyright © Cassell Illustrated

The moral right of Colin McDowell to be identified as the author of this work has been asserted in accordance with the Copyright, Designs and Patents Act of 1988.

Designer: Simon Wilder

A CIP catalogue record for this book is available from the British Library.

ISBN 13:9781844 034 798
ISBN : 1 8 4 4 0 3 4 7 9 8

Printed and bound in China

Many people have helped in the preparation of this book and to list them all would be invidious. However, there are some who must be mentioned as being especially maternal to the end product. Within Polo Ralph Lauren in New York, Ellen Maguire and Pat Christman answered endless questions and checked every fact efficiently and promptly. Tim Cook provided invaluable editorial assistance, Georgina Ford transcribed the many taped interviews and Sarah Halliwell typed the manuscript of ten at breakneck speed. I am grateful to them all, as I am to Victoria Alers-Hankey, my editor, who worked with such commitment to ensure that the book was right for us all.

The publisher would like to thank the following for permission to reproduce their material. If we have omitted anyone we apologize and shall, if informed, make corrections in any future edition.

Pages 2, 16, 19, 24, 30, 32–33, 82, 180 Les Goldberg
Pages 4–5, 44–45, 56, 59, 60, 62–63, 64, 66–67, 68–69, 70, 76–77, 78, 80, 84–85, 91, 92, 94–95, 131, 188–189, 194–195, 199, 201, 205 Bruce Weber
Pages 8, 11, 13, 20, 23, 171, 177, 196–197 Lauren Family Album
Page 15 Buffy Birrittella
Page 26 Daily News Record
Pages 173 Victor Skrebneski
Pages 36, 38–39, 50(r), 51, 53, 54, 102, 110, 121, 122–123, 124–125, 126, 134, 139, 142–143, 147, 148, 150–151, 154–155, 156–157, 158–159, 161, 165, 166, 185 Polo Archive
Page 42 Kobal Collection
Pages 48, 50(l) Tony Edgeworth
Pages 86–87 Bruce Weber staff
Page 108, 112, 116 Polo staff
Page 99 Irving Penn
Page 100 Sheila Metzner
Page 104 Dan Lecca
Page 132 Shooting Star
Page 168, 176, 181 Barbara Waltz
Page 190 Richard Corman